ADVANCE PRAISE FOR

us know that different is what makes the world awesome."
—Trisha Hershberger, YouTube host of SourceFed

....k is like a cookbook for empowerment— very practical, very easy to read, totally delicious . . . just like Emily-Anne."
—Nancy Lublin, CEO of DoSomething.org and founder of Crisis Text Line

"*FLAWD* is inspirational *and* practical."

—Gabi Gregg, fashion blogger

"In a culture where young people are consistently told that they are not 'good enough,' *FLAWD* is a guide that challenges this statement by saying, 'You *are* enough.' Emily-Anne is an important voice and leader for today's generation."
—Taylor Trudon, editor of "HuffPost Teen" at the *Huffington Post*

"I wish this book existed when I was on the brink of losing myself to the unrealistic standard of Hollywood."
—Monique Coleman, actress and global youth advocate

"The world is a better place because of Emily-Anne. She cares deeply about making each of us feel better about ourselves—flaws and all!"
—Ann Shoket, millennial expert and former editor in chief of *Seventeen*

"*FLAWD* is a collection of voices from a rising generation."
—Hannah Brencher, founder of More Love Letters and TED speaker

"*FLAWD* is an essential book at an essential time."
—Eric Dawson, founder of Peace First

CONTINUED . . .

FLAWD

How to STOP HATING on Yourself, Others, and the Things That Make You WHO YOU ARE

Emily-Anne Rigal

with

ideas and illustrations by
Jeanne Demers

A PERIGEE BOOK

PERIGEE
An imprint of Penguin Random House LLC
375 Hudson Street, New York, New York 10014

FLAWD

ISBN: 978-0-399-17403-2

This book has been registered with the Library of Congress.

First edition: August 2015

PRINTED IN THE UNITED STATES OF AMERICA

10   9   8   7   6   5   4   3   2   1

Text design by Pauline Neuwirth
Illustrations by Jeanne Demers

While the author has made every effort to provide accurate telephone numbers, Internet addresses,
and other contact information at the time of publication, neither the publisher nor the author
assumes any responsibility for errors, or for changes that occur after publication. Further, the
publisher does not have any control over and does not assume any responsibility for author or third-
party websites or their content.

Most Perigee books are available at special quantity discounts for bulk purchases for sales
promotions, premiums, fund-raising, or educational use. Special books, or book excerpts, can also be
created to fit specific needs. For details, write: SpecialMarkets@penguinrandomhouse.com.

for Papa
for seeing my dreams from
a place of yes and teaching
me the value of accepting
people as they are

Contents

you have flaws

Yes, I said it.

And I meant it.

And I'm here to represent it.

And so are a lot of my peers.

Because you're not alone with your flaws. Far from it.

Every person on this planet has a flaw. Flaws can range from something physical, something emotional, to something you just downright don't like about yourself.

Momo055650, age 16

So, who is this person jumping straight into the scary flaws conversation right off the bat? Well, it's me, Emily-Anne Rigal. I founded the nonprofit WeStopHate when I was sixteen. Now, five years later, my passion is still helping others to feel comfortable being themselves.

And flaws fascinate me. Do they fascinate you? Like, why do we have to have them and why do we spend crazy amounts of energy doing things like . . .

☐ avoiding the sight of them
☐ obsessively focusing on them
☐ hiding them from the World
☐ being intolerant of them in others

In short, why do we have . . .

OR...maybe you don't do ANy of that...

Maybe you're in a really good space when it comes to flaws. Maybe you're enlightened on the subject and you want others to feel the same kind of liberation. If that's the case, you already know that accepting what you don't like about yourself sets you free.

> It's about just accepting your flaws and just moving on with your life because there's so many more things to life than just worrying about not having the clearest skin, not being the prettiest, not being the smartest, and not succeeding at absolutely everything that you do.
> Momo055650, age 16

We're all somewhere on this spectrum. Do you know where you are?

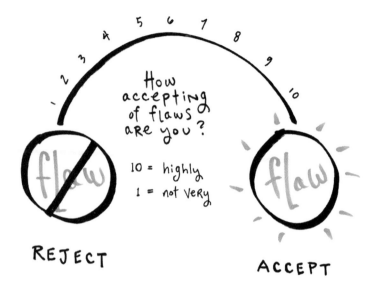

How accepting of flaws are you?

10 = highly
1 = not very

REJECT

ACCEPT

Let's do something. Regardless of where you are on the spectrum, try imagining this: WHAT IF we collectively went ridiculously hardcore in the direction of . . .

"Heck yeah, I have flaws!"

My makeup is almost always uneven. I have these really annoying fangs that even braces couldn't get rid of. I have terrible asthma that occasionally makes me look like a little bit of a wimp. Let's just say I have less than perfect skin. My hands are really chubby. And believe it or not I'm actually kind of a shy person. And as much as I sometimes don't like those qualities about myself, I know that I wouldn't be myself without those qualities. And the last thing I would ever want to do is be something that I'm not.

AidanIsWeird, age 15

WHAT IF we could all be up-front and accepting of the things we don't like about ourselves? Well, we can. It's a matter of getting a handle on how we look at these things. And that's what *FLAWD* is all about.

It's about perspective. It's about examining and playing with our perspective so that even though we live in a society that thrives on flaw hate, we can move in the direction of flaw love.

A Little Backstory

←—————————————

The *FLAWD* book came into existence because I asked my peers on YouTube to make videos answering these questions:

- Do you have any confidence tips and tricks you could share with other teenagers?

- Have you ever overcome a bullying experience?

- Will you share your story?

The reason I cared about these questions?

When I was in elementary school, I was severely bullied for being overweight. I thought I came out of it okay (after switching to another school, where my classmates accepted me, flaws and all), but apparently I wasn't *all-the-way* okay because . . .

I turned into a bit of a bully myself.

Thankfully, at my new school, I was surrounded by classmates who understood that being mean to others isn't right. The longer I knew them, the more this rubbed off on me. And gradually, I started to feel better about myself.

Once I felt good about myself, I wanted other people to feel the same. It was a lightbulb moment . . .

People who feel Good about themselves want others to feel the same.

this means they don't put others down!

And the best part about this happening to me so young? As a teenager, it doesn't occur to you that you can't do whatever you think up. You just do it.

So I created a YouTube channel. "And I'll call it . . . WeStopHate! I'll ask my YouTube friends to make short, honest, entertaining videos about their own experiences with confidence and bullying."

Almost immediately the WeStopHate channel took off. Within eight months of posting our first video (thanks, JJWeb-Shows101!), WeStopHate was the 27th Most Subscribed YouTube Nonprofit Channel OF ALL TIME.

And along with tons of video views (helloooo, ONE MILLION!) came long streams of supportive, thankful comments.

> WeStopHate is probably one of the most relevant communities for teens out there. It's basically this channel where you watch tons of other teens share their stories and combat negativity with positivity.
>
> WhatThePoo, age 17

Suddenly teens from around the world were submitting home-made videos — all of them sharing personal stories and advice and inspiration in creatively teenage ways. We began shipping WeStopHate wristbands to teens all over the country and across the globe. Word spread both online and in real life to the point where a movement was under way.

I really do hope all of you know that you are your own person and you're beautiful in that way because you're so unique. And this channel WeStopHate really helps that.

AdorianDeck, age 18

So that's the story of how a lightbulb moment turned into a life philosophy and that life philosophy turned into a movement . . . and that movement produced the little book in your hands right now!

This book can help you — regardless of your age — because while it would be nice if self-esteem issues were something you just grew out of, the reality is they're something you deal with in life until . . . you deal with them.

I'm so delighted you're reading *FLAWD*. It's filled with issues teenagers today care about. And their insights are relevant to people of all ages.

So here they are: Lessons from teens to the world. Lessons that are about encouraging us all to . . .

See yourself as perfectly imperfect.

Treat life as playfully as possible.

Think about what really matters.

Embrace all that makes you, you.

Understand influence and how to use it.

Know you can be part of a flawd and powerful transformation.

It doesn't matter whether you're a teenager or not — you're going to appreciate that the voices in this book are AWESOMELY WISE.

And funny.
And big <3-ed.
Oh yeah, and flawd.

Not a bad thing, a human thing.
↑ very

Look at You

It's okay to be unique. It's okay to be the person you are. And it's okay to tell yourself you're beautiful. Inside and out. Because you are.

DaniCaliforniaStyle, age 16

Who Am I?

When I ask myself that question, I get brain freeze. It's as if a teacher is springing a pop quiz question on me and I feel I must know the answer because it's such a simple question, but . . . "Who am I? Who *am* I? Who . . . AM I?"

For a super short string of monosyllabic words, they sure pack a punch when you put a question mark at the end of them.

Here's the problem: It's too big a question. When a question is too big, there's no way to wrap your head around it.

Who Am I?

To answer it, you need to find ways to break it down into more manageable, bite-size questions:

Who am I . . . *with my friends?*

Who am I . . . *with my family?*

Who am I . . . *when I'm imagining my future?*

Who am I . . . *when I open my eyes in the morning before the first thought comes in?*

We go around with this idea that we have "a" personality. But the truth is our personality is a very complex thing. Different aspects of our personality come out at different times depending on who we're with, what we're doing, how much sugar we ate an hour ago.

- If I saw myself as having a whole bunch of different characters inside me, what would some of the characters be like?

- If I were an animal instead of a person, which animal would I be? Why?

- If I were doing something that I really love (and I'm loving who I am while I'm doing it), what are the qualities I experience when I'm fully engaged? Might that be the essence of me?

- Making stuff is a good way to learn about who we are. If I were going to make something (anything at all), what would it be?

Okay, I'll admit those weren't really "off the top of my head." It's more like off the top of a Google search. They're good, but they don't exactly get to the heart of "Who am I?"

So how do you get there?

This little gem posted by a Facebook friend begins to get to the heart of "Who am I?"

We mistake ourselves for our STORIES.

We have STORIES,

but we are NOT our STORIES.

– Mark Matousek

All those experiences from my life? Are you really telling me they aren't actually *who I am* and instead they're something I *have*?

This way of seeing myself — as *having* experiences without *being* them — got me thinking about the other things it's easy to think we are. I mean really thinking.

The Internet lets you create a person that isn't you. I got over that when I realized that I was losing myself. And I don't want to lose myself. I have to know who I am. Who is Tommy? Who I am is not this person that I created.

JustAddTommy, age 17

So let me ask you something:

Do you think you *are* your body?

It's kind of easy to think you are your body because you look down and go:

Here I am. That's me. I'm right here.

And if you thought that (like I did), you'd be right . . . but wrong. Our bodies are undeniably part of us in the same way that our experiences are part of us. Your body is no different than your stories, though, in that . . .

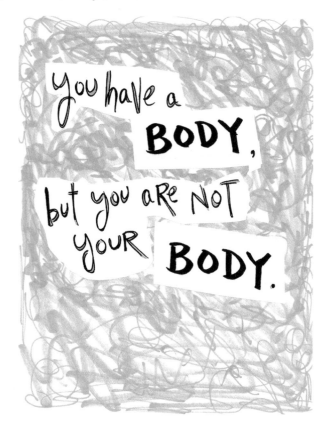

This leads to the first way you can think about "Who am I?"

YOU are made up of many things without being any one of them

If you're not your stories *and* you're not your body, are you . . .

    . . . *your name?*

    . . . *your labels?*

    . . . *your experiences?*

    . . . *your age?*

    . . . *your social status?*

    . . . *your personality?*

NOPE.

You *have* stories, but you are *not* your stories.

You *have* a body, but you are *not* your body.

You *have* a name, but you are *not* your name.

You *have* labels, but you are *not* your labels.

You *have* experiences, but you are *not* your experiences.

You *have* an age, but you are *not* your age.

You *have* a social status, but you are *not* your social status.

You *have* a personality, but you are *not* your personality.

I know . . . this seems so negative.

You're probably thinking, "I must be *something*."

And I'm here to tell you, "Yes, you are, you are a lot . . ."

... a lot Lot LoT.

• Self-Truth 2 •

you are a mystery

This will either be a huge relief to hear or . . . you're looking at the book sideways thinking, "Whaaaat?"

We live in a world where *knowing stuff* is valued above all. We love to know. We *have* to know. It makes us feel like everything's going to be okay.

But let's face it: There is so much we can't grasp. So much that is just full-on mysterious about life as a human being on planet Earth in the twenty-first century.

Bear that in mind as you ask yourself . . .

Where did I come from?

Why am I here?

What do I love and why do I love it?

Why do I struggle the way I do?

What's going to happen next?

Why did what's already happened happen?

How will I contribute while I'm here?

Why am I "me" and not "you"?

Where do I end and you begin?

It's okay if you don't know. Or if you don't *ever* know. Seriously.

"KNOWiNG"
is a moving Target.
Sometimes
we hit it;
Sometimes we don't.

And that would be because . . .

• Self-Truth 3 •

You Change Constantly

You and everything around you.

You think you know things about yourself, other people, the world, and then *POOF* . . . those things change. There's no escaping it. From the moment you're born until the day you die, things are changing.

Everything Changes. Including us. Constantly.

Since everything is constantly changing, is it possible to ever get to the end of a question like "Who am I?" and answer it?

I don't see how that's possible.

So maybe a good way to think about "Who am I?" is as though it were a game. But not a game where you try to "win" (as in, get to the end of it successfully). The goal of the "Who am I?" game would be to . . .

Keep the game going!

Keep playing "Who am I?" Because being you is a *process* — an ongoing, exploratory process where you get to find out a little more . . . then a little more . . . and then . . . oh . . . look at that, some more of me.

Even though you're a mystery — an ongoing one — you can't walk around like that's what's going on. The world we live in isn't mystery-friendly enough for that. The better thing to do (and we all do it) is put something protective on top of your mystery. Something that lets you look like your act is somewhat together even as you're figuring out who you are.

• Self-Truth 4 •

You Wear Masks

Masks. Not singular, but plural. You have a collection of them. We all do. Over the course of our life we each make and wear a series of masks. They're made out of those things that are a part of us: our body, name, stories, labels, experiences, age, social status, personality . . . all that.

You start making your mask when you're really young by taking those different things — emphasizing some more than others — and weaving them together until you end up with a mask that is a custom-crafted, designer *original.* ← Like a snowflake. ❄

> I'm an individual fingerprint. And I'm learning to accept that that is such a cool thing.
>
> KaitlynMariex3, age 16

Your mask isn't something you put a lot of work into and then get to go, "Done!" Mask-making is a lifelong undertaking due to the fact that you keep changing.

Take my life, for example. At this point, because I'm in college and I'm very interested in everything "pro-social," the mask I'm wearing — as in, the way I present myself to the world — is an upbeat, go-getter dedicated to making a positive difference.

But six years ago, I was primarily interested in creating hilarious YouTube videos. Back then, I was wearing the mask of silly teenager with a talent for talking to the camera.

> Whether you are a boy that wants to wear makeup to school and bling-y jewelry, or you're a girl that wants to wear a football jersey and Army cargo pants, it doesn't matter because you rock. You are going to rock this world whether it be in makeup like me, or you have dreams of being a doctor or a lawyer.
>
> AlyxJW, age 15

We need our masks. We really do. They're *tools* for helping us navigate the world. However, if you let yourself get tricked into thinking your mask is "who you are," then it stops being a tool and becomes a *crutch*. You know, like something you use to hide behind. It happens all the time. Thinking your mask is who you are is an incredibly easy trick to fall for.

Which is why it's incredibly important to learn how to take a peek behind your mask . . .

• Self-Truth 5 •

YOU have a wealth within YOU

If you think of your mask as something for the world to see, you're only accounting for one side: the outside. But there's the inside of your mask, too. The inside is what you — and only you — see.

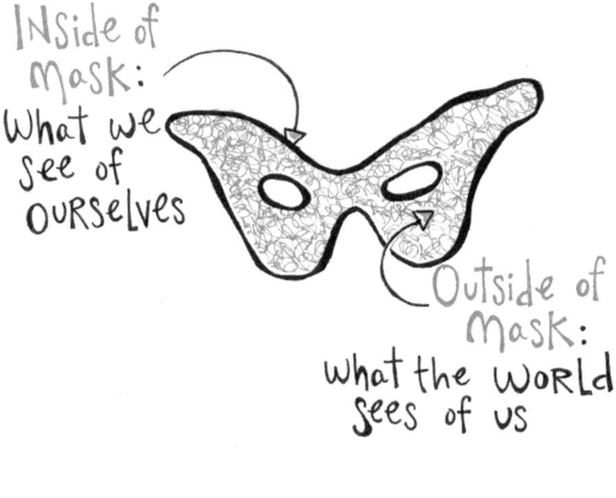

INSIDE of
Mask:
What we
see of
OURSELVES

Outside of
Mask:
what the WORLD
Sees of us

What everyone (well, not everyone, just almost everyone) suffers from is the mistaken perception that it's the *outside of our mask* that really matters because that is what's seen by the world.

But it's the opposite, actually.

The *inside of your mask* — what you're dealing with on a daily, moment-to-moment basis — is the side that matters most.

Why?

Because it's loaded.

There's so much inside you that you couldn't tap into all of it even if you tried. But you should try. There's tons in there — y'know, things like your emotions, imagination, hopes, and dreams and just your ordinary, everyday ideas, too — all of that will tell you about who you are.

Want to tap into some of it? I know a way. It's very easy.

First, grab a pen and a piece of paper or sit near a computer. Then quiet yourself and use the blank page or screen to blab what's inside of you right now. Just let it rip. Stream-of-consciousness style. Fast, furious, and fun. What's fun is you don't know what's going to come out . . . until it's out!

To help you get the idea, here's a peek at one of my blab sessions:

Ready?... Set... BLaB...

 April 6, 2008

umm. well im 14 i live in williburgg. i love myy friends. i talkk wayy too loud. and too much. but i love it. im crazy about quotes and i love to text msg. on my enV. i cant wait untill i can drive. i love beaches. and swimmingg. i tend to talkk about tv. and i always say stories more then once. my room Is always messy. and i like facebook wayy more then myspace. i usallyy double myy "y"s. i like to do musicals. i prefer TV over movies for sure. i love starbucks. im crazy about radio. im gonna be a radio personality. i really believe im a superstar. i take alot alot of pictures. i type kinda fast. i know really random stuff about MTV. my dogs name is lola. and i used to have a hedgehogg. i hate stupid movies with stupid jokkes. i love my bestfriendsforever. im sometimes rlyy into takkingg risks and other times im wayy too scared. i love meetingg new people. i can be shyy around guys i like. i wish i wasnt tho. but i cant help it. im prettyy good at keepingg secrets. but i do have a big mouth. my name is rly unique. and so am i. i crave attention. theres nothingg i can do about that. i cant help it. i just love it. i love when i know people at a store. and i rly like change.

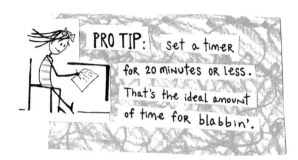

PRO TIP: set a timer for 20 minutes or less. That's the ideal amount of time for blabbin'.

My blab session went on for pages, but that gives you the idea. As you can see, it's not about writing well; it's about tapping into all that's in you. When you read back over your blab session, you might be amazed, like I was: "Wow! There really is something to seeing your thoughts in words on a page."

It's because by putting them on paper, your thoughts are now outside of you. You're given a tangible glimpse into your insides in a way that you can't through just thinking about it.

But — *major* but — you must be willing to . . .

tell the TRUTH

Oh, I know. It can be scary to tell the really true truth about ourselves . . . even just to ourselves. Maybe *especially* to ourselves. For some reason, it can feel embarrassing to say in so many words what we *really* feel, what our heart's desire *really* is, what we *really* don't like about ourselves, what we're *really* going through.

But if you're not willing to tell the really true truth, then blabbing it out onto a page doesn't do anything. Telling the truth is the only way you're going to be able to tap into the wealth within you.

What's the point of being something you're not?
There's no point at all.

DeeFizzy, age 15

After shining some light on "Who am I?" it's clear to me now: It's not a question meant to be answered. It's a question meant to prompt other questions that can help us check in with ourselves. Reflect on things.

You reflect on things by considering them. Things like what you see, feel, think, do . . . and "are." Take any one of them and shine a light on it. Look at it. Think about it. Question it.

Who Am I?
I'm still figuring it out.

These are some of the questions I've come up with for reflecting on things, along with my short-version answers. (Long-version answers are good, too, if you have the time.)

How's it going?

I don't know. I think it's going okay.

Have any mysteries turned into discoveries?

I played disc golf for the first time last week. Who knew I was naturally good at throwing a Frisbee!

Have any changes taken place in me recently?

I have a newfound appreciation for my mother's sense of humor. She is *funny*! (Has she always been so funny?)

What's my mask currently made up of?

Well, thanks to writing this book, a smart new literary-type thread is getting woven into it.

How's my inside doing?

On a scale of 1 to 10, I'd give my inner life . . . mmm, a 6½ right now (angsty details to follow in my personal journal).

How's my outside doing?

In preparation for my upcoming dentist appointment, I'm flossing regularly.

Do either one of them need extra attention?

My insides are begging for a date with my journal. Gonna go blab it out . . .

NOW
it's
your
turn...

- How's it going?

- Have any mysteries turned into discoveries?

- Have any changes taken place in you recently?

- What's your mask currently made up of?

- How are your insides doing?

- How are your outsides doing?

- Do either one of them need extra attention?

Go ahead, tell the really true truth and blab it out.
Keep going with it and see where "Who am I?" takes you.

All the mixture of experiences that you've had? You're
the only one that's had the mixture of those
experiences. I mean, that's something super valuable.
AdorianDeck, age 16

Increase your Perspective

Count in your life how many things are bad and count how many things are good. Not just the major things, everything in your life. I can almost guarantee you that you have more good than bad. Your problems aren't that big of a deal when you think about it in perspective.

FloppyStarfish, age 16

Isn't perspective just the way we see things? We look, we see. That's our perspective. No biggie.

Except, it's a very big biggie. You begin to get *why* when you consider that *what you're looking at* and *how you're seeing it* are **two entirely different things**.

When I think about them being two different things, it clicks with me that perspective isn't meant to be passive . . . it's meant to be active. Actively messed around with so it can be kept healthy and strong and ever increasing. To help me remember this, I've come up with . . .

THE
THREE
KEY
P's

· Perspective

· Play

· Practice

It's a heck of a combo. I'm eager to share how the Three Key P's combine, but the thing to do first is look at each one individually. Each one on its own is a very big biggie that can help you deal with with flaws . . . and pretty much everything else in life.

• Key P 1 •

Perspective

The dictionary describes it as . . .

> **perspective**/per-**spek**-tiv/ (noun) — a particular attitude toward or way of regarding something; the way you look at things; a point of view.

Then there's what "They" have to say about it. "They" — that hard-to-locate crowd of know-it-alls — say . . .

"Perspective is Everything."

But you can't believe everything They say. You need to question the things They say. Is perspective *really* everything? Maybe it's more like a large percent of everything without being absolutely everything.

But no. I looked into it, and They *are* right on this one. Perspective is everything. Primarily because it determines the quality of your whole life. It's such an extreme concept, we need a moment to let it in:

The quality of your whole life is determined by this . . .

Perspective, it's a quality-of-life issue.

When thinking about the quality of life that you'd like to have, consider the two far ends of . . .

The "How To Look at Things" Spectrum

How do you FEEL when you LOOK at yourself?

...all tight and UNhappy OR ...Nice and Relaxed and OpeN?

Here's a way to get a read on where you actually are on the spectrum:

Take an aspect of yourself that concerns you and look at it. Maybe it's your health or your finances or your great wish to be more _____ (fill in the blank).

As you look at this concerning aspect of yourself, notice how you feel. Would you characterize it as a kind or an unkind feeling? It could be mixed feelings. But whatever it is, notice it. These feelings give you a clue as to how you tend to look at yourself.

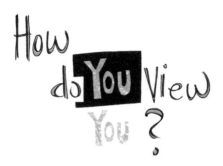

How do **You** View You?

As far as perspectives go, how you view yourself is Perspective Numero Uno. Nothing is more important. Really, nothing. How "you view you" holds the number one position because . . .

How You see yourself... is how **You** see ...everything.

We should pause to let this one sink in, too: *How you see yourself is how you see everything.* Can you think of a time this has played out in your life — in either a positive or a negative way?

As I consider it, I'm thinking about a time when I felt bad about myself. I can see now how that colored everything.

It was after I decided to go to a new middle school because of the bullying I'd been enduring at my old school. As you may remember from the little bit of WeStopHate backstory I shared, in the new school I was finally accepted and liked for who I was, but the messages I'd gotten about myself while being bullied were still with me: Being fat made me NO GOOD.

So, how do you think I saw and treated the things around me? Like they were no good, too . . . even though they were good! I remember this time so vividly because I was acting in a way that makes me cringe to admit.

I went from being on the receiving end of mean girls to becoming a mean girl myself. I started doing things like teasing others (*"Just kidding!"*), secretly hoping it would make them feel no good about themselves, too.

"If *I* have to feel no good, then *you* should feel no good, too." Seems weird, but that's mean girl logic for you.

Thankfully the behaviors my new and supportive friends were modeling gradually started rubbing off on me. Over time their influence led me to go from feeling "no good" to "so good" about myself. And then, how do you think I saw and treated the things around me? That's right. Like *they* were so good, too.

If we all just liked ourselves, the world would be perfect.

HannahTheDreamer100, age 15

Your turn: How do you view you, and by extension, how do you view . . .

. . . *your friendships?*

. . . *your daily life?*

. . . *your belongings?*

. . . *your surroundings?*

. . . *your . . . whatever else matters in your world?*

You don't need to answer these right now. Give them some thought over the next couple of days while you're experiencing them . . . and see if there's any connection between how you see (and feel about) yourself and how you see (and feel about) these things in your life.

᪻   ᪻   ᪻

Perspective is not straightforward stuff. There are a lot of moving parts. And it's not always possible to see everything we need to see from where we stand. Sometimes we need to ask someone "over there" — a trusted someone — for their perspective on what we're in the middle of.

We Sometimes ∧ Need HELP with OUR PeRSpective.

If you're ever "lost in the sauce" of your own perspective, do yourself a favor and get an outside eye.

Sometimes when you look at a situation too close it can seem like everything is going wrong.

STHsquared, age 18

Here's a time when I couldn't see the forest for the trees, and I got the kind of help I needed.

absolute CoNfUSioN and UNCeRtaiNty

Working on WeStopHate is my idea of a good time, which is one of the main reasons my social life doesn't get enough attention. My sophomore year of college I decided I was going to solve this problem by joining a sorority. I chose five sororities to rush: the one I really wanted to get into and four backups, just in case. I was looking forward to enjoying an instant circle of wonderful new sister-like friends. Fingers crossed I'd get a bid from my first choice.

Shockingly, not one of them invited me back to the following round. It had to be a mistake. An oversight. What else could it be? Ugh, such an embarrassing problem to have to deal with. So I had my best friend call Greek Life (pretending to be me) to tactfully bring the oversight to their attention.

No. No mistake.

How could this be? I mean, I was 100% perfect for what they were looking for. Or . . . what they *said* they were looking for. It turns out I was 100% *not perfect* for what they were *really* looking for. Which was "a look." A look that a top-heavy girl who loves horizontal stripes didn't have.

It was truly devastating. On a lot of levels. But the ego level mostly. I'm used to getting what I go after and . . . I wasn't getting it. Worse, there was NOTHING to be done. Except call people and cry.

Besides my mother, my friend Jeanne is someone who I'm comfortable being completely humiliated in front of. So I called her. Blubbering.

The only thing I wanted to hear was, "OMG, you're right, your life is OVER!" but instead, Jeanne was saying something like, "Yes . . . yes . . . *AAAND* even things this tragic pass."

Hearing that helped me arrive at a new perspective. Other things in my life *had* felt that bad (sometimes even worse) and none of them had lasted.

It does get better. Actually, I don't know because I'm still a teenager and it's like . . . HECTIC! But you hear from people that are older and they're like, "Yuh, it goes away."

MisterKenzie, age 15

And that *is* how it went. The tragedy passed. Less than a month later I was sent an email about my school's Social Justice House — a living space for students interested in social issues and activism and positive change. It was right up my alley. I applied and got in.

Life is full to the brim of second chances, so take one, at least one.

DiamondInTheRufff, age 16

If the way you look at things is, in fact, everything (and it is), and how you see yourself is how you see everything (and it is), then *how you look at things* is something worth getting good at.

And what's the way we get good at things?

Practice.

Practice, practice, practice . . .

ractice

They say, "Practice makes perfect." ←

But They're a little off the mark with a statement like that. They're emphasizing something minor about it as though it's the whole point of it. The point of practice is NOT to make things perfect; it's to make things POSSIBLE.

The beauty of practice is the way it changes things. With enough of it, practice changes things into habits. Good habits or bad habits depending on what you're practicing. Good habits make life a lot easier and are highly worth the time and energy it takes to create them.

PeRfect is
the opposite of flawd
and something I have
veRy little inteRest in.

Think of an obvious habit like brushing your teeth and its more challenging counterpart, flossing. They weren't always, but are now (I hope!) habitual for you. Daily practice transformed them from less-than-fun into easy-to-get-done.

And boy, do we love easy-to-get-done.

But it's our love of easy-to-get-done that can get in the way of taking on a new practice. In the early stages of taking on something new, it doesn't feel easy-to-get-done. Leaving things the way they are? Very easy-to-get-done.

Since we're talking about practice as it relates to our perspective, let's look at something perspective-related that's easy to leave the way it is. It's something we all do a lot more than we might want to admit:

Seeing something JUST ONE WAY.

Seeing something JUST ONE WAY is easy because it happens pretty much all on its own. It happens based on our conditioning. Without even trying, we automatically have a first impression of something.

But how about being able to look at something MULTIPLE WAYS? Getting good at this is worth the effort it requires if for no other reason than it makes you less of a bore.

Looking at the same thing more than one way is like this . . .

Stick figures have a way of making things look really simple. But try it.

Take anything. Anything at all. Notice the way you think about it.

Got it? Now come up with two other ways of looking at it. Maybe that was a snap for you with the thing you chose to look at. But trust me, there are some things in life that will be on the impossible side for you to look at from multiple points of view.

I speak from experience. In fact, as recently as last week I couldn't do it. I was listening to a new boyfriend share his perspective on poor people.* I really want to be able to keep liking him because he's so cute and *reallllly* sexy . . . but as soon as his worldview hit my ears, all of my energy had to go toward keeping my eyeballs in my head and remembering how to breathe. The additional energy it would have taken to attempt to see things from his perspective just wasn't there for me. Though goodness knows, I was trying.

Really worth noting, though, is how differently things went just a few days later when I overheard my friend's sister say the homeless just need to "get their act together." Instead of losing my cool, it somehow occurred to me that her news sources must be very different from mine. I think that happened, in part, because of my earlier (heroic but failed) attempt at seeing things other than the way that makes the most sense to me.

---

* I'm not betting on this one working out.

Hard as situations like these are, they're a primo opportunity for making giant strides when it comes to seeing things other than your one, usual way. But you have to be willing to *try*. You don't have to be at all successful; you just have to try. *Really* try.

Trying matters more than actually succeeding because of what They say about "anything really worth getting good at." They say 10,000 hours. You wanna do something well? You're gonna have to put in 10,000 hours of practice.

I'd much prefer that They were wrong on this one, but based on a lot of people's experience with putting the time in and *not* putting the time in, I do think They're right.

However, I also think you can expedite the process. Heavy lifting is worth time-and-a-half in my book. And trying to see a point of view that doesn't at all meet with your approval? *That* is heavy lifting.

Practice makes Possible.

To keep yourself from giving up when unhelpful thoughts strike — thoughts like, *It's just too hard* . . . *10,000 hours, who has the time?* . . . *I'll never get there* — think about art.

Yes, art.

Think about what it takes to look at something and draw it on a page in 3-D. That's the *art version* of perspective. We're very used to 3-D in art nowadays — like those incredible chalk drawings on the sidewalk that make you think there's a crater with a dining room inside it and you're one step away from falling into it.

But 700 or so years ago that kind of perspective in art didn't exist. Everything was flat. Perspective took a long, long, long time for artists to master. That's why they're called masters. And even though artists now know how to create perspective, it still requires practicing like crazy . . . even to be *bad* at it.

Which is where the spirit of play enters the mix.

It's amazing what
sidewalk artists
can do.

• Key P 3 •

There isn't one thing you could do that playfulness wouldn't make better. Look with playfulness and you'll see better. Practice with playfulness and you'll progress better. It's the nature of play. Play is fun. Having fun is better than not having fun.

The question then becomes how to get good at playfulness. You're in luck: It's the exact opposite of the 10,000 hours approach to getting good at things. We all have play inside us. So you don't need to put in an absurd number of hours to be good at play — you just need to connect (or reconnect) with what's already right there inside you.

Check in with how in touch you are with your playfulness. Review your life (eyes closed, please) as you ask . . .

- How good was I at playing when I was a kid?

- How good am I at playing now?

- How good am I at noticing when I'm losing contact with playfulness, and then calling it back again?

As I think about these questions, elementary school comes to mind. I was the youngest in my class (December birthdays, woot-woot!), so I tended to love things that my peers had already outgrown. But I wasn't a kid who faked not liking things I really *did* like. So even though Britney Spears was no longer cool, I would still pretend to be her. This landed me squarely in the uncool kids' camp . . . but, hey, I had fun there.

What are they doing that's cool? They're being just like everybody else, oh that's cool. They're doing things that they think other people will like, but people who choose to do their own things are cool. In my opinion.

FloppyStarfish, age 16

Yes, in fourth grade I had a real talent for making things fun. Like if I were cleaning my room, I'd pretend to be the host of a TV show. I was also the guest. I'd interview myself and explain to the viewers at home how to clean a room.

Today I don't interview myself anymore, but I do sing along to country music as I clean and it's the same amount of fun. So I still got it.

If you can play (and otherwise be yourself) without caring about being judged, that's a good sign. It's a sign your view of yourself is in very good (playful) shape.

If you live your life as if no one is watching, then you are actually who you are, and you know what? You're awesome.

TimsVlogs, age 19

Keeping each one of the Three Key P's in good shape will mean taking each one of them on like a practice . . . which is exactly what each one of them is:

PeRSPecTive is a **PRacTice.**

PLay is a **PRacTice.**

PRacTice is even a **PRacTice.**

Up next I'll share how to *combine* the Three Key P's so you can start actively messing around with how you're looking and seeing. Combining them into one practice may sound highly advanced, but you can do it. The secret is keeping the emphasis on the fun one: Play.

Are you ready to connect play to everything?

Connect Play to Everything

Whenever I have a blah day, I will usually jump up (I've probably been sitting). I'll jump up wherever I am and I will do a little jig, do a little wiggle, do a little "Here we go!"

Eden Sher (@EdenSher), age 22, ABC's *The Middle*

Decide right now if you'd like to . .

. . . or not.

YES? Read this chapter and learn how to play six different perspective shifters.

NO? Skip ahead to any of the other chapters. There's plenty to dip into.

You picked YES! Good move. Get ready to life hack.

Life hack — any trick, shortcut, skill, or novelty method that solves an everyday problem in an inspired, ingenious manner.

Connecting play to everything is a life hack, because it includes the everyday little (and big) "problems" that aggravate, annoy, and upset us. Connecting play to those things? That takes skill, all right!

If you want to master connecting play to everything, the first thing to do is make sure you're playing with all the easy, obviously playful stuff — as much and as often as you can.

Play with kids, animals, friends. Get crazy with colorful Post-its to organize the tasks on your to-do list. Start your day by hardcore lip-synch-voguing to "Ain't No Mountain High Enough" as you make coffee (Diana Ross version).

Play like it's your job. Play like you're the boss. That's how to make it so play will be available to you on an as needed basis. As *needed*. The way you'll *need* it when you find out your crush doesn't feel the same way. Or when your mom won't stop talking while you're trying to watch Netflix. Can you play with that?

The trick to mastering this skill:

That's it. It's not that you're going to enjoy what's aggravating or otherwise upsetting you. You're going to enjoy what play asks of you. It asks — no, it *requires* — that you be irreverent — that you be sufficiently disrespectful of the way things usually get handled, that you feel free to do them a different way.

You can *enjoy* this!

PLAY is irreverent.

it shows a LACK of RESPECT FoR what USUaLLy gets TAKEN SERIOUSLy.

Admittedly, I'm a little anti-establishment so I probably enjoy this kind of thing more than I should. But my number one way to practice playing with my perspective is with a status-quo buster – a status-quo buster that's like an industrial strength cleanser. It's perfect for the most hard-to-remove stains on our society.

· Perspective Play 1 ·

WHAT IF. These two words are the most powerful perspective tool available to us. And so easy to use.

Just stick WHAT IF in front of anything you can think of, and coming up with new possibilities becomes child's play. This is because WHAT IF isn't a real question. It's hypothetical. Hypothetical means it's not really happening, and what isn't really happening doesn't threaten us. Ideas that don't threaten us are ideas we can entertain.

Try it. Say WHAT IF and watch what happens . . .

What if...

there didn't have to be hate in this world?

What if...

we could get the food industry to stop putting weird, harmful, addictive chemicals in the foods we like most?

What if...

what we're being told is all wrong?

What if...

I stopped doubting my opinions on global issues and expressed them more confidently?

Your Turn:
What if...____?

QUESTION: Does asking WHAT IF open you up to the possible?

· Perspective Play 2 ·

I'm going to be honest: When asking WHAT IF, my very first thought in response to it is often a negative one because the scenarios don't feel realistic. I've got this irrational, anxious, skeptical Naysayer inside me going . . .

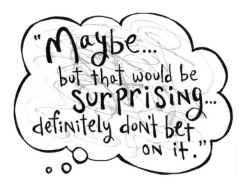

This is when you bring in the backup. You (politely) interrupt your inner Naysayer with . . .

"Why NOT?" and "Who Says?"

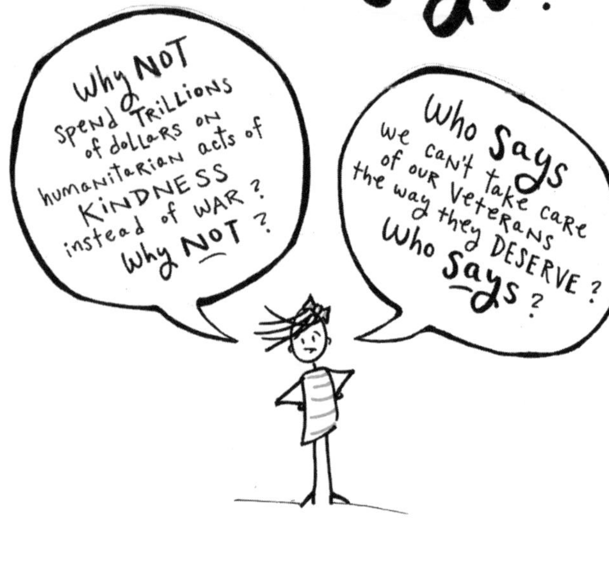

If you're like me, your inner Naysayer is really good at its job by now and you're going to have to keep countering its nays with WHAT IF, WHY NOT, and WHO SAYS for a while.

Just keep with it because . . .

• Perspective Play 3 •

The next way I connect play to everything was inspired by a story my friend Adorian Deck shared in his WeStopHate video:

> I lost my dad less than six months ago and it's a very sad thing. Especially when it's a month before your senior prom and two months before your graduation. And my dad doesn't see any of that. But I've become so much stronger of a person by the fact that I appreciate so much more. Like what you have with your family, and just in general how lucky you are to have what you have.

If we are "just in general lucky to have what we have," why do we take so much of our good fortune for granted? Why aren't we able to see and appreciate what is right in front of us? Or what is right *inside* of us?

The
"Seeing & Appreciating
what is Right in front
of us" spectrum

#1 would be where the things about us that are

Outrageously good, but get Outrageously overlooked, are.

NONE — ALL

Given the choice, how would you rather be in relation to your everyday good fortune?

Me? I like having appreciation for my everyday good fortune, so to help me with that I use . . .

STEP 1. Look at What You've Got

Look and make a long list of all the super-easy-to-take-for-granted things in your life. The smaller the better.

So I went home and I wrote up a list — 60 pages of single lines — of everything I could think of that my body did or that I appreciated about my body. I got granular: breathing, blinking, heartbeat, waste management, everything.

Ragen Chastain (@DancesWithFat), body positive activist

STEP 2. Take It All Away

Imagine those things gone, taken away, lost . . . *forever* lost. Feel the grief, the loss, the fear.

> I chop my leg off. In my mind.
>
> SassiBoB, age 25

STEP 3. Give It All Back

Now give it all back to yourself. Each thing, one at a time. Do it slowly so you can appreciate each one's specialness. Really receive it.

> I mean little things in life, like a sunny day, a pretty looking cloud, a nice little bug on the ground, everything.
>
> ClaireLawlorrr, age 17

QUESTION: Does doing this change your appreciation level?

• Perspective Play 4 •

Move Backward
...into the Past

Do you remember when you were a little kid, the only thing that mattered were sleepovers in the basement with a tub of ice cream . . . you could ride around your block on your racer scooter and be the coolest kid in town . . . you could watch Arthur at exactly 3:30 everyday like it was nobody's business . . . you could avoid vegetables like the plague . . . you could avoid the opposite sex like it's the plague . . . you could take your shirt off at any point in time and nobody would bat an eyelash . . . you didn't have any inhibitions. . . . And then sixth-grade rolled around and girls started getting boobs and insecurities and guys started getting deeper voices and egos. Things started changing and you started worrying about what you were wearing and what you were saying. You were becoming acutely aware of what other people thought of you. Try going back to when you were a little kid, try watching an episode of Arthur. It really helps, I promise.

WhatThePoo, age 17

This way of playing with our perspective involves time traveling!

Thinking back to your childhood is another way to gain a fresh perspective. Childhood is a good place to go if you've lost touch with being able to goof around and not care what you look like . . . and you want it back.

QUESTION: Is there anything about how you were as a kid that you miss?

• Perspective Play 5 •

Move Forward
...into the future

What inspired this way of playing with perspective was a post that went around the Internet for a while called "The Top 5 Regrets of the Dying." A nurse who cares for a lot of dying people wrote down what the dying people said during their last days. It got me thinking about the kind of regrets I'd like to avoid having. Thinking about this kind of thing pre-pre-PRE-deathbed gives you time to do what it takes not to end up with regrets.

The #1 most common REGRet: "I wish I'd had the courage to live TRUE to myself, not the life others expected of me."

In August 2009, I was diagnosed with leukemia. It was a turning point in my life. It was when I stopped and said to myself, "Life can be taken away from you in a second." You don't want to be lying there with regrets. I need to help at least one teen realize that they are so amazing.

AlyxJW, age 15

QUESTION: Based on how you're living now, if today were your last day of life, what would your biggest regret be?

When you're on your deathbed, what do you want flashing by in front of you? Do you want your memories to be of you sitting in your room crying over how lonely or fat or ugly you are? Where you hate yourself, your school, your parents, and everything else around you? Or do you want to remember all the smiles you created on people's faces? The laughs you shared. And the things you've accomplished. A great life with laughter and fears and the way you fought through it all? You decide. And decide NOW because life is short.

GummybearsRaining, age 16

• Perspective Play 6 •

Jumping around in time can inform and increase your perspective, but staying put in the present is THE place of all places to be . . . if you can get there.

The present is a strangely elusive place to enter and stay for a while. But don't fret. I have a way of connecting play to everything that also helps me connect to the present moment. And even stay there for more than a second.

I do it by listening. For sounds. Because sounds are in the present moment. Listening for and to sounds puts you in the present moment with them.

To make listening fun (because I admit it, I resist the present moment), I came up with three "zones" and the game is to identify which zone a sound is coming from. The zones are:

- Inside my body

- Inside the room I'm in

- Outside the room I'm in

Sounds from...

inside my body

inside the Room

Beyond the Room

As I listen, I bounce around from zone to zone — just with my ears, not my whole body. In fact, I'm mostly very still as I do this.

"Oh, that's my belly gurgling . . . that's the sheet against my leg as I shift positions . . . that's a car in the distance . . . that's the refrigerator . . . that's my breath inside my nose . . ."

Sometimes I don't hear anything except the ringing in my ears, but I'm ready for whatever sound will show up next. Try it. It really is fun. Eyes open or closed, your choice.

I think it helps you stay calm and relaxed and see things clearly.

Alyson Stoner (@AlysonOnTour), age 20, *Cheaper by the Dozen*

QUESTION: Can you play with the three zones of sounds even as you're doing other things?

✻ ✻ ✻

These six Perspective Plays are really just to get you started in connecting play to everything. Off of these, you're going to come up with tons of your own ways to play.

Remember, play is a way of relating to the things in and around you. How much play goes on in your life is up to you. You are The Decider. You *always* get to say.

Think...
Then Think
again

You are the only person who can define who you are, not anyone else.

ProjectCaritas, age 17

"Redefining What Defines Us." That was the original title of this chapter, before I started wondering about those words.

Redefining what defines us...
What does define us? ... What is it
to be defined? ... What's the definition
of 'define'? ...omg, that's funny...
but... what is it?

define
verb • de·fine • \di-ˈfīn\
to set forth the meaning of

So . . . *WHO does that?* Who "sets forth" *our* meaning?
I am so sorry to be the one to tell you, but . . .

it's the media.

> We start comparing ourselves to television and magazines at a really young age. Girls and boys can suffer from this thing called low self-esteem because they don't match up to the Hollywood standards.
>
> CreeCaptures, age 15

When it comes to the social side of media, I'm as big a lover of it as the next Facebook junkie. But there's no way around it: The whole media thing goes over-the-top the same way junk food goes over-the-top. But I also love junk food.

junk food

uses the perfect combination of salt, sugar, and fat
to excite your brain and get you coming back for more.

the media

uses the perfect combination of images, sound bites, and
celebrity to excite your need for what they're pushing.

> You see people in magazines and they always look so
> perfect and they're airbrushed, whatever. Everyone's
> like, "No, they photoshopped that." OK, but I still
> want to look like that, y'know?
>
> JasonLeeSegal, age 16

If you're like me, you probably think that media has an addictive effect on other people, but not you. That's the Third-Person Effect — the phenomenon where people think the media influences everyone except them and their children.

NEWSFLASH: It's impacting ALL of us. It gets the neurons in our brain to (repeatedly) fire off the belief that we lack pretty much everything, *but* if we can just spend enough money, we'll be able to make ourselves "all better."

Being defined as NEVER good enough? If ever there were something worth redefining, it might be that.

But how do we do it? How do we go about redoing definitions that are ubiquitous (everywhere at once) and subliminal (operating below the threshold of consciousness)? How do you redefine *anything*?

Before you can redefine, you've got to pay a visit to . . .

RE-think
RE-consider
RE-imagine

. . . and every other RE on the map.

re-Play!
re-dream
re-view
re-consider
re-visit
re-think
RE
re-evaluate
re-cover
re-imagine
re-deem
re-assess
re-Value
re-define

Mind-mapping is great for opening your mind up to connections that don't seem like they're at all connected. I was mind-mapping those REs when a YouTube video began replaying in my head. (Oh! RE-*PLAY!* Adding, adding . . .)

The video was on Columbus-ing. Columbus-ing is when white people "discover" stuff that has already been discovered. What was striking me as noteworthy wasn't that white people are great revisionists (oh, but we are!); it was how brilliant adding "–ing" to something is. You can just create your own verb . . . give it a definition and . . . voilà! Term coined. And if it's good enough, it might just catch on. Maybe even get wiki-ed.

Ba-rillllliance!

I do not love how bursts of brilliance get followed by, "Yeah . . . very clever, but . . . HOW IS IT DONE?" What an inspiration zapper. Like, "What? I have to *think* now?"

What I do love, however, is how the subconscious goes to work on questions you can't answer and helps you find the answers.

So, when I wasn't even thinking about how to RE anymore, my subconscious popped this into my head: "What *is* Critical Thinking all about anyway?"

If you take a minute to peruse the "Critical Thinkers" diagram, you'll see that Critical Thinking has what it takes to look at things with intention *and* information *and* your best interest at heart.

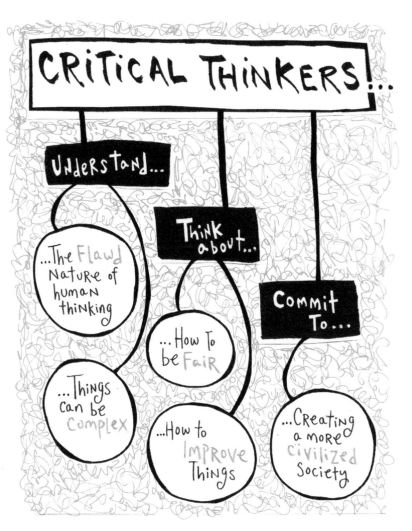

I love what Critical Thinking is about!

I love it so much I'm Columbus-ing it.

Yup, I'm appropriating it in its entirety. It's bold, I agree, but Critical Thinking is *that* good.

But what a lousy name. So uninviting.

It's okay, I'll just do what some white people who discover what's already there do and give it a little RE-brand. RE-name it, RE-frame it, and RE-introduce it to the world.

RE-vitalizing something so very needed will be a service to humanity. I don't know when or why, but somewhere along the way Critical Thinking fell out of fashion. There is not nearly enough of it going on today (in my humble opinion).

Just watch any one of the "news" channels. You'll see professional people — hosts and invited guests — with differing opinions discussing something by talking *at* and *over* each other. The person who talks the loudest, the longest is . . . uhhh, most intelligent?

Should it happen that the point of view you agree with comes out on top, it can be kind of entertaining, but . . . not really. Really, it's sad — it models something uncool. It models intolerance. And rudeness. And ignorance.

WHY NOT some collaborative analyzing? WHY NOT some re-construction of the thoughts being presented?

Maybe because we don't know *how*.

Well, now *I* know how! And it is my pleasure to give you . . .

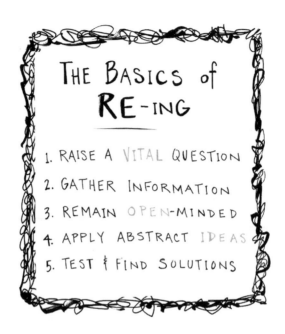

THE BASICS of RE-ING

1. RAISE A VITAL QUESTION
2. GATHER INFORMATION
3. REMAIN OPEN-MINDED
4. APPLY ABSTRACT IDEAS
5. TEST & FIND SOLUTIONS

RE-ing is a step-by-step process that lets you take an in-depth look at something. It allows you see what you already know and also find out what some of your other options are.

Want to try RE-ing on something worth looking at?

· RE-ing Step 1 ·

Raise a Vital Question

What makes a question vital? I don't really know because what can seem like a "good" question can turn out to be an obvious one. And what can seem like a "stupid" question might end up being very thought provoking. As the Queen of Stupid Questions — seriously, I am! — here's my advice:

When searching for a vital question (a question really worth exploring), ask every kind of question and see which ones stick to the wall.

~~FUNNY~~
~~stupid~~
~~clever~~
~~original~~
~~thoughtful~~
Ask ~~smart~~ ~~good~~ Questions.

ALL KINDS OF

Do my flaws define me? ❀ What else is there to life other than what's "wrong" with me? ❀ Do I overfocus on my flaws? ❀ Does hating . . . resisting . . . denying and otherwise not being okay with flaws use up too much of my energy? ❀ What is the best way to be in relation to a flaw? ❀ Do the flaws I notice in others that bug me most have anything to do with me? ❀ How do I handle having physical flaw X? ❀ How do I handle having emotional weakness Y? ❀ Is having flaw X worse than being dead? ❀ What's inside my flaws? ❀ What's to be learned from my flaws? ❀ Why do we pretend our flaws don't exist? ❀ Why do we put either too much or not enough attention on our flaws? ❀ Are flaws bad? ❀ Or is the unkind, hateful, intolerant, judgmental attitude that accompanies them the real problem? ❀ What would a life without any flaws be like? ❀ What are flaws . . . and WHO SAYS? ❀ What kinds of flaws are there? ❀ Is the perspective I have on flaw X at all playful? ❀ Is it possible to be playful with my flaws? ❀ Might flaws be the raw material of growth?

Out of all my questions above, what gets my attention is "What are flaws . . . and WHO SAYS?" I know it could be considered a stupid question, but as the Queen of Stupid Questions, I say we go with it!

RE-ing Step 2

Gather INForMaTioN

This can be as simple as keeping your eyes and ears open for what you want to explore. Or you might do it more actively: Surf, cut, paste, take notes.

Whichever way you go about it, be prepared. Because once you have a vital question on your radar, you'll immediately start seeing and hearing tons of relevant info. You'll wonder if it's trending . . . and in your universe it *is*.

what aRe FLAWS ...aNd who Says?

Dictionary Says . . .

flaw /flô/ noun — **1.** An imperfection, often concealed, that impairs soundness: *a flaw in the crystal that caused it to shatter.* **2.** A defect or shortcoming in something intangible: *They share the character flaw of arrogance.* **3.** A defect in a legal document that can render it invalid. **4.** To make or become defective.

Survey Says . . .

I have my flaws, you have your flaws, they have their flaws. Each person has their strengths and their weaknesses and that's what makes them special.

ThatOneBrandonKid, age 17

I'm a super awkward person. I am the awkwardest of turtles. I'm also pretty high energy. Some would argue aggressively happy but really I can't help it, it's just the way I am. I like to smile and I'm just not good with social skills. Once in a while, I will get comments like, "Girl, listening to you hurts my ears." This used to really bother me until I realized something: these people don't know me.

HeyThere005, age 17

I have really big teeth and the ones at the bottom are really crooked. I'm not exactly the most muscular or manly 17-year-old in the world. Not wearing glasses gives me a headache. I'm a black person but I suck at basketball. These are all things I've been made fun of for my whole life at school, at home, and on the Internet.

Couchpotatokid05, age 17

But all those silly things that they think are your flaws are actually what makes you the most beautiful of all.

ItsAntoniaWithAnA, age 16

Personal Experience Says . . .

Throughout my teen years, what I wanted most was a boyfriend. I would willingly change aspects of my personality to please who-ever I was dating at the time. Last summer, I went out with some-one who constantly got annoyed with me for taking photos to post on social media. He made me feel like this was a flaw. Now I realize I want to find someone who will accept silly little things like this about me. I haven't found him yet, but that's what I'm looking for.

Literature Says . . .

Have you ever heard of a heroic or tragic flaw? The main character in a story has one. He or she has it because if they started out perfect, there'd be no story. Without a really good flaw, a hero has nothing to overcome. There's no reason to change, grow, or transform.

Plus, if they don't have some kind of weakness or blind spot or imperfection, then we can't relate. We're not going to care about a hero who doesn't have something "wrong" with them.

without
CHaNge
gRowth
TRANSFORMATION
you have no
~~StoRy.~~ life

Wise Friend Says . . .

My friend Mark Matousek teaches memoir writing and self-inquiry, so I asked him for his thoughts on flaws. He said:

> Flaws are basic human imperfections. Things we all have. No big deal. They're an idea — an idea that doesn't measure up to what you think "should be" true about you. There's really nothing wrong with flaws, except that you don't approve of them. That's the real issue. Not accepting them puts you in conflict with yourself. And when you're in conflict with *who you are*, you'll create conflict in your world.

That idea is so similar to the WeStopHate philosophy!

Same idea, two ways:

When you're in conflict with yourself, you'll create conflict in your world.

People who feel good about themselves want others to feel good about themselves, too.

Random Philosopher Says . . .

I was recently YouTubing the Swiss philosopher Alain de Botton, for no reason other than he's very entertaining. So when I heard him say this, it practically bit me . . .

> Korean ceramics, like Japanese ceramics, has a philosophy behind it related to the acceptance of imperfection in life. The glazing is *on purpose* not perfect. And yet it's attractive. And that's a very hard thing for our age and our society to hold onto.

WOW. It sent me in search of what's up with Japanese ceramics. And what's up with it is Kintsugi.

Kintsugi is the Japanese art of repairing broken ceramics with gold glue and making sure the gold glue really shows. They highlight the imperfection because they see it as gorgeous — as a creative addition to the pot's life story. They think that when something has suffered damage and has a history — that makes it more beautiful, not less.

IN 21st CENTURY WESTERN civilization imperfections lessen Something's Value.

IN 12th CENTURY Eastern civilization imperfections make something MORE PRECIOUS.

• RE-ing Step 3 •

Remain Open-Minded

This isn't so much a step as it is a do-it-all-along. As you're gathering information, take care not to judge it on its way in. Just let it in. That's what it is to be open-minded.

I have somewhat of a hard time with this. I've already made up my mind about a lot of things, mostly without even realizing it. So anytime I find myself judging what I'm hearing, I call to mind an epiphany the guy who writes raptitude.com had one day . . .

"Strong Beliefs are NOTHING to be PROUD of."

Strong beliefs are just the intensity with which you resist questioning yourself.

That's why they're nothing to be proud of. Strong beliefs are the opposite of an open mind.

The question then becomes, are there any strong beliefs you have that are preventing you from being open-minded as you explore . . .

I have one giant belief that gets in the way of this exploration. It's the belief that when it comes to my flaws, I *know* who says.

I say.

I say (quite strongly) that I'm physically unacceptable in certain ways. Being the one "who says," it doesn't occur to me to question it. And anyone who tries to tell me differently? I'm going to roll my eyes at them.

What really ought to be done with the things we don't want to let in is to look at them even more closely than the things we're okay with hearing. Because it's the things we resist that have the most to tell us about ourselves. By a long shot.

When I take a close look at "Honey, there's nothing 'unacceptable' about the way you look," I'm shocked to see that I have the world divided into things that can be accepted and things that can't *based on nothing more than how they look!*

Yeah. Weird.

• RE-ing Step 4 •

abstract Ideas

(apply)

Abstract thinking is playful thinking. Everything we did when we were connecting play to everything involved abstract thinking. It allows you to zoom out of yourself and look at what you're doing as though it were a movie.

So, let's try Moving Forward into the Future to explore "What are flaws and . . . WHO SAYS?"

Imagine you're in your nineties. You have bladder control issues and chronic hip pain. The ninety-two-year-old you is sitting there thinking back to when you were the age you are now. You're remembering how you were always upset about something . . . what was it? Oh yes, that no matter how hard you exercised, the underside of your arms never looked toned enough. As a ninety-two-year-old, you look at your arms and think, "They *work*, I love 'em!" You pop back to today and get it that what makes flab on your arms a flaw is thinking it is.

Good job time traveling! To be ninety-two when you're not is to think abstractly.

RE-ing Step 5
Test & Find Solutions

We've just gone through all that gathering up of information and open-mindedly thinking about it, so when we ask ourselves the question again, we can see what we think now.

what are FLAWS ... and who says?

For me, it's this:

Flaws are (still) things about me that bug me, but now I'm willing to consider . . .

What if...

being bugged by them is actually a good thing?

What if...

in dealing with having flaws, it makes us better, richer, more thoughtful people?

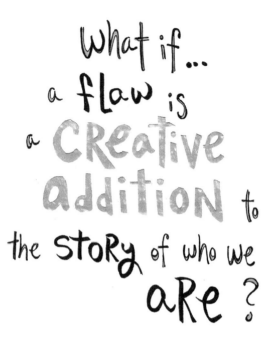

What if...
a flaw is
a CREative
addition to
the StoRy of who we
aRe ?

That's my new take on them: My human imperfections make me more interesting and more precious, not less.

Test it out in your own life. Walk around with these ideas. Go find some more ideas. See what feels true to you.

Once you've gotten into a habit of RE-ing, you'll want to do it all the time. Because thinking for ourselves is *fun!* And maybe more important, the ability to think for ourselves is *power*. It's the power to live your life according to the definitions you think up, you try out, and you decide on.

EmbRace the Whole of you

You know what I do? Girl, I embrace it!

xSamiSDx, age 16

Let's talk about embracing yourself. Seriously embracing yourself. Seriously embracing yourself is about accepting the whole of you. Accepting everything that makes you, *you*. The whole of you wants an embrace like that. Seriously.

This means EVVVVVVVERRRRRYTHING (E-V-E-R-Y T-H-I-I-I-I-I-I-I-N-G . . . EVERY SINGLE THING) about you.

Knowing all that is included in this "everything" is an undertaking, to say the least. I personally haven't been able to get my head around my "everything" just yet. But maybe you have. If so, you're either well on your way to enlightenment or you're bluffing yourself.

Here's why I think it's such a challenge to wrap your mind (and arms) around "*everything that makes you, YOU.*" In three words . . .

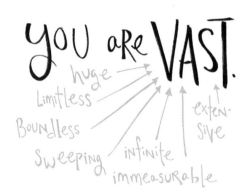

Remember this Self-Truth from Chapter 1?

Being vast is a big contributor to that. It's a little overwhelming to think about being a vast mystery, so let's focus on what *is* known about us. Fortunately, there's a lot in the known column.

Let's look at the things we do know about ourselves, piece by piece . . .

· Known Piece 1 ·

The Physical you

Your body is vast.

Anatomy and physiology aren't my thing, so when it comes to the extent to which the human body is a miracle, I know relatively little. But I think these facts and figures I got from a search for "amazing facts about the human body" give us a glimpse into how astonishing our flesh suits really are:

Your nose can remember 50,000 different scents. ❋ An adult is made up of 7,000,000,000,000,000,000,000,000,000 (7 octillion) atoms. ❋ The human eye can distinguish about 10,000,000 (10 million) different colors. ❋ In a lifetime, your brain's long-term memory can hold as many as 1,000,000,000,000,000 (1 million-billion) separate bits of information. ❋ There are 100,000 miles of blood vessels in an adult human body. ❋ An average person produces about 25,000 quarts of saliva in a lifetime, enough to fill two swimming pools. ❋ Everyone has a unique tongue print. ❋ Human bones are, ounce for ounce, stronger than steel. ❋ Your heartbeat changes and mimics the music you listen to. ❋ There's more bacteria in your mouth than there are people in the world. ❋ Every day your heart creates enough energy to drive a truck for 20 miles. ⁕ If uncoiled, the DNA in all the cells in your body would stretch 10,000,000,000 (10 billion) miles — from here to Pluto and back. ⁕ When you take one step, you are using up to 200 muscles.

That's a whole lot of awesome . . . and it's just a fraction of what's going on. *And it's YOU!*

I wish I knew sooner how awesome my body was. Now that I'm getting older I realize, "Oh my God, it's this incredible vessel that I have to carry me through this lifetime. And it fights off diseases and infections, and it breathes on its own." It's pretty incredible.

Olesya Rulin (@OlesyaRulin), *High School Musical*

• Known Piece 2 •

The Non-Physical you

Next up, there's the non-physical part of you — the part you can't see or touch. But what *can't* be seen or touched is no less real than what *can*.

The non-physical piece is your inner life: your emotions, thoughts, imagination, intuition, observations, greater understandings, and so much more.

The more rational thinkers among us tend to resist the concept that what is invisible to the eye counts as much as (if not more than) what can be physically seen.

Just like once upon a time people were convinced that the earth was flat and the sun revolved around us, a day will come when people will say, "There was a time when people were convinced the physical world was the most important of all."

> A lot of people think of money and cars and clothes as success. In reality, those things can be taken away very fast. So I think the main thing is what's inside. So if you're a happy person, if you're content with yourself, if you trust yourself, if you're humble, if you love yourself, if you love everyone around you, and you're positive about your life, you are successful.
>
> Coy Stewart (@CoyStewart), age 15,
> Nickelodeon's *Bella and the Bulldogs*

Known Piece 3

The "Not Separate from Anything" you

This next piece goes far beyond the physical and non-physical pieces. It's the piece that connects you to everything else because . . .

This may strike you as counterintuitive because when you look around, you *see* that you *are* separate from other things. Except modern physics has been telling us (for quite a while) that separateness is an illusion. A giant optical illusion.

Luckily, you don't need to get a degree in quantum physics to be able to see through the illusion. You just need to be able to go out and look at the interrelationship of nature (or if you're not into nature, look at any aspect of the world at all). If you really look, you can't help seeing how dynamically interconnected everything is.

As an example that needs our attention: Colonies of bees all over the world are dying right now. You don't need to be Einstein to figure out "no more bees, no more pollination, no more plants, no more animals, no more mankind," but according to urban legend, he actually is the one who said that. Conversely, if we take care to address what's causing honeybees to die en masse, pollination continues . . . and so do plants, animals, and mankind.

Not being able to see something doesn't make it any less true. Everything *is* connected to everything else, making our "personal vastness" not personal at all.

The truth is we belong to each other and the earth.

Holding on to the idea of separateness is messing us up. It makes us believe it's possible to do things like . . .

- Take all the valuable parts out of the earth without it affecting the whole.

- Make overly simplistic statements about poverty and addiction without looking at society as a whole.

- Do something to one part of our body without concern for what that will mean to the whole of it.

A QUIZ

1. Can we **fully understand** everything that makes us *who we are*?

YES ☐   NO ☐   MAYBE ☐

2. Can we **accept** everything that makes us *who we are*?

YES ☐   NO ☐   MAYBE ☐

1. NO, we can't *understand* it all.

2. MAYBE we can accept all that we are. It's not a given, but it is possible.

· Next Step ·

Embrace*

(((ALL THREE
PARTS)))
of
Y O U

* Love + accept

The "everything" part of self-acceptance is what trips most of us up. Accepting what's easy to accept about yourself is a good place to start, but it doesn't quite count as self-acceptance. Because it's not technically who you are.

You're not goodness and light and sunshine and rainbows ONLY.

You're dark corners and scary nights and prickly patches and thick scabs ALSO.

So how do you begin to embrace those less-easy parts of yourself?

Self-Accept Step 1

Face It

To accept anything, the first thing to do is face it. The good news is you don't have to *like* something to face it. You just have to be a little courageous, a little daring.

I discovered a few years ago that nobody could possibly hate me as much as I hate me. It forced me to address all of the things that I hated about myself. I thought of them all. If I can take, oh whatever, "I have bad eyes, I'm obtrusive in every single situation, I make people uncomfortable, I, whatever, have body image issues that are so stupid," if I can look at that, what's anyone going to say that I haven't already thought of?

Eden Sher (@EdenSher), age 22, ABC's *The Middle*

Just face it.
It's not THAT bad.

flaw → ← me

To face what you don't like about yourself, I recommend drawing two circle faces that are facing each other (it's all about where you place the eyes). One is you and one is the thing you don't like about yourself. They're two characters now. They can talk to each other now.

I mean, you're going to be the one to write down what they say, but it will be there for you to hear after you draw the circle faces. I'll do it so you can see this technique in action.

The first thing I came up with is "I don't like that I overthink things."

But that felt a little whatever, so I drew two more circle faces. What came out next is that more than I don't like the fact that I overthink things, I really don't like that I'm bigger than most of my peers.

Being less-than-okay with being big led me to think about how I don't like it that I don't go out. The whole process is exhausting to me. I sometimes resent the amount of time I need to veg out. My idea of a good weekend is being at home alone in my pajamas.

Face it,
you like to stay
(in your Pj's.

I'm in my
pajamas
85% of
my waking
hours.

⌣ I do.

Thinking about my pajamas led me to thinking about how I also don't like it that I don't have a hobby.

Face it,
you don't have
(a hobby.

I don't.

This never bothered me until a friend told me I needed one. So I went on Google to find a list of hobbies and see what my options were. But none of them fit me. Not liking how I don't have a real hobby put me in touch with how jealous I can be of people who have what I want.

Okay, now we're talkin'!

If you were to double-dog-dare me to say the thing I don't like most about myself, it's that even though I've won more than my fair share of awards, I still get jealous when I see people I know winning things I think I could have been winning. This is really hard for me to accept about myself. But there it is.

Can I accept it? Not *reallllly*. Can I face it? I just did.

You may be a little bit overweight, or your hair doesn't go the way you want it to, or your clothes don't fit right. Or you don't have huge boobs, or maybe you have huge boobs and you hate them. Maybe you have tons of freckles, or maybe you have that one mole on your face that you wish would go away. Maybe you have bad acne, or some kind of skin disease. Maybe your teeth aren't straight, or maybe you have a gap.

TaylorrScreamsRawrr, age 15

YOUR TURN:
Face it,
you...

Having faced it, you're now in a good position to . . .

· Self-Accept Step 2 ·

Embrace It

> Gleaking is when a jet of saliva shoots out of your mouth, and sometimes onto other people. And it's really awkward. It's usually involuntary, but it happens to me all the time. I do a million other things that make me different than everyone else. I just have to embrace it.
>
> Adri411, age 19

Imagine wrapping your arms around something. Imagine it's such a warm, inclusive hug that nothing gets left out of it. Now imagine the hug nobody likes giving or getting. The stiff, really-not-into-it hug.

Now imagine all of what you don't like about yourself in front of you . . . suffering . . . in need of a good hug. It's time to see if you can . . .

HUG the HELL out of YOUR flaws.

Hell. I know it's a bad word, but I'm using it anyway. I'm using it because Hell is a place and heck isn't. Hell is the place nobody wants to go, but we all do go there when what causes us to suffer just won't let up. Things like insecurities that eat away at us. While suffering with insecurity, we're transported to Hell . . . without ever having to leave the living room.

> Insecurities are little devils that will always, always eat at people.
>
> Danielle Chuchran (@DaniChuchran1),
> age 21, *Dr. Seuss' The Cat in the Hat*

Is there a way out?

Yes, there is.

Hug it out!

Try it with one of your insecurities. Imagine giving it the warm, loving kind of hug. An embrace that's filled with no shortage of . . .

• Side Step •

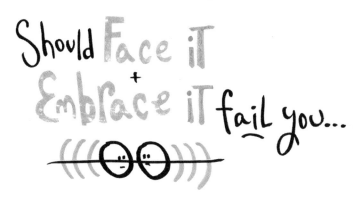

I really wanted Face It and Embrace It to be an all-purpose solution to everything that's less than easy to accept about ourselves. A one-two punch . . . that even rhymes!

But what if you're able to face, but not embrace? That could happen. If you find yourself face-to-face with an unembraceable, here's an alternative . . .

• Self-Accept Step 3 •

Do Nothing

Yes, nothing. Just let it be.

It sounds like the easy way out, but that's only because you haven't tried it yet. Do Nothing means being able to say, "I give up trying to change this flaw. I may not be able to embrace it, but I'm not going to reject it either."

do nothing = SURRENDER to things just the way They are.

Can you do that? Can you let the truth of something you don't like about yourself just *be*?

To "Face It and Do Nothing" is to Understand...

- The spirit of *who you are* isn't changed by this flaw.

- You're big enough for this flaw to exist without it changing *who you are*.

- The existence of this imperfection can deepen *who you are*.

I'm thinking that Do Nothing may be a good step to slip in after Face It and before Embrace It. Maybe taking the time to Do Nothing could make Embrace It less challenging. This is all trial-and-error-type stuff, not an exact science. The steps will vary from person to person and from flaw to flaw. Be playful as you try these things out and you'll see what happens.

Here's another follow-up to Face It you may want to try . . .

· Self-Accept Step 4 ·

Re-frame It

> Sometimes it could be negative, but sometimes that
> same thing could be really positive, too. I think that
> there are many aspects of you that are like that.
>
> Josie Loren (@JosLoren), ABC Family's *Make It Or Break It*

Re-framing is when you see that a thought you're having is charged with a lot of challenging feelings so you say to the thought, "You're not helping. I'm going to find a more positive alternative for you."

I used re-framing with some thoughts that were holding me back. As a naturally loud person, I thought, "I'm no good at being quiet. Always being loud is humiliating!" I still experience embarrassment when I remember sitting in the hallway of my dorm, talking and laughing on the phone and finding out later that everyone in their rooms wanted to strangle me the whole time.

To re-frame it, I think back to when being loud turned out well. Like when I won the TeenNick H.A.L.O. (Helping and Leading Others) Award. I was sitting in a large audience at the MTV Studios and Lady Gaga unexpectedly asked me a question about WeStopHate. When I re-watch the episode, I see that when I said, "Everything that Lady Gaga stands for is what we believe, too," everyone could easily hear me. Re-framing can turn what we consider to be a weakness into a strength. When I'm disturbing everyone on my floor, my loudness feels like a weakness. When I get called on to answer a question and I'm easily heard, it's a strength.

> If I positively use these things I don't necessarily like about myself, I can make myself better instead of tear myself down.
>
> JillianLovesFilm, age 16

The whole weakness-that's-really-a-strength thing is so common it should make us feel very differently about our flaws. The history of achievement is filled with stories that go . . .

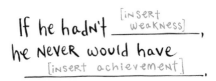

If he hadn't _[insert weakness]_,
he never would have _[insert achievement]_.

If he hadn't gone deaf,

he never would have given up conducting and performing and focused on composing.

Beethoven

If she hadn't contracted a childhood illness that left her deaf and blind,

she never would have inspired us all with her determination to communicate.

Helen Keller

If she hadn't gotten her heart broken,

she never would have written songs million of girls (including me!) could relate to.

Taylor Swift

If she hadn't been so severely bullied in elementary school,

she never would have created WeStopHate to help people accept who they are.

Me

Re-frame It is a powerful RE that asks you to think about what you don't like about yourself . . . and then think again.

What is your . . .

"If I hadn't _____, I never would have
_____."

Or another way to ask it . . .

"If I weren't _____, I wouldn't want to
_____."

Having gotten to the end of the chapter that set out to EMBRACE THE WHOLE OF YOU, I think what we've arrived at is . . . it's a tall order. And not always possible. But it's okay because we also discovered that "embrace" isn't our only option.

Maybe instead of EMBRACE, we should say BE IN A HEALTHY RELATIONSHIP TO . . .

And instead of THE WHOLE OF YOU, it should be AS MUCH AS YOU CAN MANAGE.

BE in a healthy Relationship to as much of you as you can.

That *is* good. But I'm not going to re-title (which would mean re-work) the whole chapter now. Hindsight is allowed to be constructive without being time consuming. It's enough to thank the wrong title for sending us off on a good exploration that produced these takeaways . . .

The **VAST** "everything of you" is already there and gets **revealed** bit × bit.

YOUR JOB is to make the **revealing** easy.

How To Make
it easy...

1. Let yourself be in awe
   of all that is known
   and UNKNOWN.

2. Look things square
   in the face.

3. love what you can.

4. do Nothing as needed.

5. be on the lookout
   for goodness.

6. get into a healthy
   relationship with
   as much of you
   as you can.

Use Influence Responsibly

Influence yourself by surrounding yourself with supportive people and supportive images and messages. Surround yourself with people who are confident and will tell you why you are beautiful.

Gabi Gregg (@GabiFresh), age 24,
body positive fashion blogger

The world is round. It's why there's a circular nature to a lot of things. Influence, for example, is circular. It's something you both *get* and *do*.

It's good to be able to notice how you're being influenced (what you're allowing into your mind) as well as what kind of influence you're being (what type of energy you're putting out into the world). Why? Because influence has power. A lot of power, it turns out. The power to shape us . . . and the world.

When I think about the importance of influence, a story about the Buddha comes to mind. The Buddha was a very enlightened man who lived 2,500+ years ago and is responsible for giving us — among other things — the Middle Path: the idea that it's about balance, not extremes.

The story I'm thinking of is the one where the Buddha is on his deathbed and his cousin Ananda (who was with him all the time and wrote down everything he said) is with him. Ananda wants to get whatever final bits of wisdom out of the Buddha while he still can so he asks, "What's the single most important thing if you're interested in leading a holy life?"

And do you know what the Buddha said?

" Whom you SURROUND yourself with."

That's the single most important thing.

I think that's a pretty incredible answer. However, even though it was said by an enlightened man, you still have to ask, "Is it true?"

Recently, I read a piece about Chris Peterson — a researcher who contributed a lot to the field of positive psychology. Before he died, he was asked, "Of all the research you've done on well-being, what is your most significant finding?"

And do you know what Chris Peterson said?

That's his most significant finding.

"Other people matter" confirms what the Buddha said about whom we surround ourselves with being so important. Chris Peterson's take on *why* it's important is this:

> Other people matter because so much of our happiness is dependent on others.

Think about the "other people" in your life. Think about the ones who are most important to you. Think about how your life would be without them. To really get how different your life would be without them, play the Morbid Trick on yourself:

Imagine your most important "other people" GONE. Imagine it until you really feel what you're imagining.

Feel how different life would be without them?

It's okay, you can give them back to yourself now.

And guess what?

To someone who's not you, you're their "other people." You matter in the same way to them.

When it comes to who your "other people" are going to be (the people who will influence you) and the "other person" you're going to be (the kind of influence you will be) . . . these should be actual *choices*.

Choices that are *conscious*.

I grew up in a small high school with a small group of friends. Everyone had their group of friends and you didn't really leave your group of friends. Most of the hate, the bullying, the drama, the tears I suffered in high school were from my group of friends. Well, finally, one day I decided that I didn't like what my friends were doing. I didn't like how they were treating me and I started making new friends. It was very difficult. But in the end I was very happy with my choice. It made the last couple years of high school a lot more fun.

Nayders07, age 18

So let's first look at being conscious recipients of influence — being super picky about what we're letting in.

• Influence Strategy 1 •

Use Responsibly

One of the first things to do when choosing who influences you is to identify encouraging people. This may mean going out and searching for them, or simply recognizing that they're already there.

Encouraging people are the loving, supportive, inspiring people who can help you become the best version of yourself. You want them around you because their qualities will naturally rub off on you.

> I live my life by the 60% rule. Picture this: you're sitting in your room by yourself. At that moment you're at 60%. Now, whatever enters your life, can either increase or decrease that percentage. You should surround yourself with people and things that make you a better person. If there's something or someone in your life that makes you feel less than 60%, you should get that thing or person out of your life. You'd be better off without that person or thing.
>
> ItsAyyLucky, age 18

So who are these people?

Role Models

There are many people in my life who have qualities that I'd like to emulate. But until I met Jess Weiner when I was fifteen, I didn't know anyone who embodied so much of what I aspired to in life.

Jess is a self-made businesswoman who helps empower women and girls around the world by educating and advocating for them. She has also gone through her own struggles with weight and body image just like me. When I met Jess, there was suddenly a person in my life who was doing all the things that I hoped to do once I got older. I had the perfect role model.

When I created WeStopHate, she turned into a mentor.

I call her
mama mentor.

Jess helped me set the vision and encouraged me to keep thinking bigger. I didn't let challenges stop me because I wanted to make her proud. Knowing she had my back also helped me feel confident.

Jess introduced me to all kinds of inspiring people, but what inspired me most was knowing her — someone who was living the kind of life I hoped to one day live as well.

To find your own Jess, you first need to find your own self. This means being able to authentically answer "Who Am I?" When you know what you want and what you value, and you come across your own Jess, you'll know it.

Once you've found a role model that's right for you, do not be afraid to put yourself out there and ask for the help and guidance you need.

❋ ❋ ❋

On the other side of things, you may have people currently in your life who bring you down rather than lift you up . . .

MoMENTaRiLy INESCaPabLE PERSON

You may have someone who's less-than-wonderful in your life. By all means, be nice about it, but . . . show them the door. Or you find the door.

Unless, of course, you *can't*. Then what you're dealing with is. . . .

A (momentarily) inescapable person. Someone whose presence in your life you have no control over (right now). Maybe it's a family member, a teacher, a classmate, a boss, a coworker . . . you know, someone situational.

When it comes to people like this in my life, I find coming up with the right WHAT IF can help a lot.

WHAT IF when [momentarily inescapable person] makes me want to scream, I breathe in and out five times instead?

WHAT IF my time with [momentarily inescapable person] is actually precious and I just need to look to the positive in this?

WHAT IF a day truly will come when I won't have to see [momentarily inescapable person] anymore?

The people who say mean things about you are people you're not going to have in your life for much longer. So just work on yourself and work on making yourself feel good.

JJsHeart, age 19

The Virtual World

In my mind, as we discuss people who influence us, I'm only seeing IRL (in real life) people. I'm forgetting to account for how much time we spend on screens and with buds in our ears.

What you connect with in your virtual world needs to be chosen with the same kind of conscious care as IRL influences. Think about it. What's coming in through those open windows? What are you watching? Reading? Listening to? Taking in?

Is it encouraging, loving, supportive, inspiring?

If not, shut those windows.

※　※　※

Take full advantage of the best things others have to offer. There's so much of it that you can be good and *gluttonous* about it. At the same time, steer clear of the influences that are just "ehhh" . . . or straight-up bad. There's so much of that, too.

Are we clear on "choose consciously"?

Okay, moving over to the other side of the equation . . .

· Influence Strategy 2 ·

apply generously

Once you've allowed in the best influences, you're not going to be able to help it: *You are going to want to share.* If acted on, this need to share turns into the way you help shape the world.

> There's a lot of things that you can focus on, but a lot of the times what's super, super overlooked is how powerful of an influence you can be in someone's life.
> Strawburry17, age 19

When everyone has the same kind of power available to them, it's easy to miss the fact that it *is* power.

Newsflash: Influence is power. And we all have it.

Influence =POWER

We all have the power of influence because we all have people whose lives we touch. The people whose lives we touch (in any way) are within our "sphere of influence." When you act on any of the many opportunities there are to be a helpful, soothing, or in any way a positive influence in the lives of others . . . you're shaping the world into something better.

Be generous that way. Share the good you've got going on. Share a lot of it.

EVERYbody has a Sphere of Influence.

How are you using yours?

How *do* you influence the people around you? As a force of good . . . or not? Being a force of good in the world is pretty straightforward. It's a more or less simple matter of connecting with the better aspects of our human nature — our virtues — and bringing them out into the world.

I've collected a bunch of human virtues. Take a look at them; see which ones jump out at you as very "you." As in the ones that you use most often and most naturally.

Which human Virtues do you recognize as "yours"?

Wisdom CURIOSITY Honesty Social emotional personal intelligence

Love of Learning Empathy COURAGE

INTEREST CReativity Optimism enthusiasm

GENEROSITY Zest ENERGY Awe

LeaderShip Wonder PURPOSE

Love HUMANITY

bravery OPENNESS FAITH JUSTICE

COMPASSION fairness

BaLaNCE TEAMWORK

humility forgiveness

Prudence PlayfulNess Loyalty

FYI: There's no limit to how many you can have.

The virtues you think of as very "you" (because you use them most often and most naturally) are your Signature Strengths. Your Signature Strengths are your keys to applying influence generously because . . . well, because it's easy to be generous with what you've naturally got a lot of!

It's also worth paying attention to the virtues that you don't think of as especially "you," but that make you go, "Ooooh, *that one* . . . I'd like more of *that one*." Those could be "you," too — but in a more latent, not-yet-signature kind of way. Who knows? You may find yourself being able to be generous with them somewhere down the road.

But either way — whether they're a strength of yours right now . . . or not yet . . . or not ever — it's very, very good to be *thinking* about human virtues, just in general and as much as possible. Because of what lies at the *other* end of the spectrum: human vices and the grip they can have on us.

Ha-Ha! No Pun intended!

Vices are the unhealthy habits of mind that get in the way of our happiness. Things like feeling entitled to more than we need . . . being intolerant to the point where we hate . . . letting our insecurities cause us to be petty and dishonest.

They're no good. But bizarrely, we live in a world where those are the very things that get celebrated and rewarded. Look at the way Wall Street rewards dishonesty and greed. Look at the way our political system nurtures dishonesty and divisiveness. Look at the way TMZ celebrates mean-spirited pettiness (in the name of honesty).

We need to be actively counteracting crap like that. We counteract it by reminding ourselves of what's really important: human virtues.

Human virtues and our ability to use them to influence the world positively . . . That. Is. Important.

Influence positively. Influence generously. Counteract the crap.

When I lived in New York, if it was raining and I had my umbrella and I'd see someone that didn't have an umbrella, I would try and walk with them. One day I was walking home and there was an old man with a cane walking down the hill who had no umbrella. I was like, "Do you want to share?" He was like, "Okay, thank you." 92-years-old. The nicest, kindest man. We started talking about how he'd lived in my neighborhood forever. When I walked him to his door he didn't thank me for the umbrella, he thanked me for the company. Moments like that, it's just a reminder of how refreshing and great it can be to let other people in.

Allison Carter Thomas (@AllisonCarterT),
MTV's *Girl Code* and *Awkward*

• Influence Strategy 3 •

Play your
Signature Strengths

Want to explore your Signature Strengths at the same time you use them to influence the world (responsibly and generously)? Here's a game to do just that:

The Signature Strengths Game

In four easy steps:

Step 1. Identify your *favorite* Signature Strength.

Step 2. Look at how you *ordinarily* use it.

Step 3. Think up ONE creatively *simple* way to use it that will influence someone else positively.

Step 4. Actually really do it.

To get you going, let's play with one of my Signature Strengths as an example:

Step 1. My personal favorite Signature Strength is empathy. I'm easily able to put myself in other people's shoes.

Step 2. I use my ability to be empathic to avoid fights. I consider the other person's perspective rather than only thinking of my own.

Step 3. Thinking creatively for a minute, I could see using empathy to positively influence someone this way: When witnessing two friends disagreeing, I offer to mediate since I can see where each one is coming from.

Step 4. Having come up with it, I actually really do it.

The Boost Effect

Not only does the person you've chosen to positively influence benefit from this exercise, but there are benefits (scientifically proven benefits) for *you*, too:

When you use your Signature Strengths in new ways, *your* well-being gets a boost. It's actually measurable (don't ask me how).

Signature Strengths + used in new ways = a well-being boost

Go find somebody that looks sad or is having a bad day and give them a compliment. You know, it could be like, "I like your hair, I like your shoes." Or it could simply be like they're sitting alone at lunch and you go sit by them. That will not only make that other person that you helped out feel better, it will make you feel better. It will raise your self-confidence and your own teen-esteem. So go make somebody else's day.

Ricky Dillon (@RickyPDillion), age 17,
Internet personality

The Ripple Effect

No less science-based, but maybe a little less measurable, is the Ripple Effect that goes on within the Signature Strengths Game.

It's possible you're going to be able to observe the positivity that comes of your good deed . . . but it doesn't stop there. There are going to be *other* positive effects as a result of it that you won't ever see. And then there are going to be what *those* positive effects bring about . . .

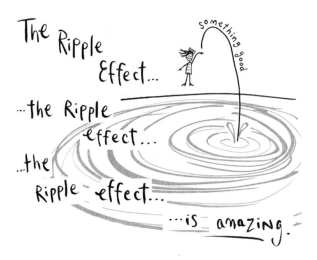

The Ripple Effect...
...the Ripple effect...
...the Ripple effect...
...is amazing.

something good

The Ripple Effect of the tiniest good deed can't be known. But imagine if we *could* see it rippling out. The interconnectivity we'd get to witness would amaze us. We might even faint, we'd be so amazed. Then we'd come back to our senses and start taking good deeds *way* more seriously.

> The ripple effect of a genuine smile is incalculable.
> Monique Coleman (@GimmeMoTalk), *High School Musical*

By using your Signature Strengths in new ways (which boosts your well-being) to do good deeds (which also boosts your well-being), your sphere of influence is increasing *exponentially* (boosting countless others' well-being).

There it is in action: The generosity of generosity. Generosity (so generously) increases itself. All you have to do is set it in motion.

It's that easy, that efficient . . . that hard to argue with.

• Influence Strategy 4 •

Avoid Traps

Of course, it's entirely possible to be using influence in reckless and irresponsible ways, too. Ways that aren't helping anybody. Ways that set a negative Ripple Effect in motion. Are you doing any of these?

Mean Speech

> They tell us when we're younger that sticks and stones will break our bones, but words will never hurt us. Sorry to break it to you, but that was the biggest lie anyone could have told you.
>
> DiamondInTheRufff, age 16

Gossip

> If I could think of just one thing in the world that's just so pointless, it would be gossip. Who really cares if Judy's makeup is lopsided today? Or Bill went on a date with Sherry? I found that when I sat there and talked about people, I thought that it was making me feel better about myself, but really it was just making me look like a mean person.
>
> AidanIsWeird, age 15

Self-Sabotage

Some people surround themselves with the wrong kind of people. You don't even realize you're doing it. The people I used to surround myself with weren't good people. Now I have friends that like me for who I am.

Nathizzz, age 16

False Superiority

"I am just too good for you darling, I'm just too good, you know?" Please, don't be a prima donna. It's just an act that you're putting on every single day. One day it's going to break.

CorttneyDunkin, age 18

Bullying

I've been cyber bullied for over two years. I'll just take a sample of something that was said to me: "Don't you remember? No one likes you. Remember Friday when you were all alone? I'm not trying to dis you, I just hate your guts like everyone else." I'm still hurt by it. Your stupid decision to make fun of me changed who I am.

DancerProductionsx3, age 16

Stereotyping

> I used to be putting out all of this hate and then getting
> back hate and feeling terrible because I didn't know
> why I was being hated on. I was judging people. If I
> saw someone with glasses, I would think they were a
> nerd. If I saw a girl with a skirt that was four inches
> above her knees, I would just instantly think that she's
> a slut. If I saw a guy wearing a football jersey, I would
> instantly think that he's a jerk. And I would make these
> assumptions based on my past experiences with
> people that do these things and act like this, but it
> doesn't mean everyone is like this. Now I wear glasses.
> I wear football shirts . . . but I'm not a jerk or a nerd.
> Although I am kind of a slut. No, not really.
>
> ThatOneBrandonKid, age 17

If you are engaging in any of these toxic, obnoxious uses of influence, you've got a little work to do . . . on you. Fortunately, the one person you have the most influence over is yourself. Use that influence to up your game.

Try using the Signature Strengths Game to override any bad habits you may have. Because that's all they are: unhelpful, unhealthy behaviors that somehow, somewhere along the way gained traction.

Do what it takes to get into a new and improved groove. To make it fun and easy for yourself, do this . . .

Influence Strategy 5

Be the Best artist

There was once a giant piece of graffiti on the side of a building in downtown Manhattan that said . . .

For a long time I thought, "How conceited."

Now I think, "How self-inspiring."

You try it out. Try influencing yourself (generously) by thinking of yourself as an artist.

Because you are. Everyone is.

We are
all artists at
being alive.

As an artist at being alive, treat everything as though it's an art form.

Because it is. Everything is creative.

Look at all the things it's possible to be, do, see, feel, experience, think about . . . That's your palette. Use it to create thought-, action-, habit-, behavior-, intention-ART . . . Create ART you could live with if you had to see it every day.

Because you do. Your ART becomes part of you.

Once you start being an artist about influencing yourself, you'll find . . .

There are so many things you can do to influence yourself and a lot of them are Really simple.

I just DANCE!! :) • I get dressed up, listen and dance to music • making other people happy makes me happy. & I'm not just saying that to sound corny. It really does :) • I always feel so good after I watch westophate videos! they're amazing! <3<3<3 • write down everything you love on post-its & stick them around your room and locker to remind you to keep smiling! • i talk to my friends or hang out with my friends when im down. • I go to piano lessons :D • being a band geek (: • I love making people laugh (: • make someone else's day! i put on a nice dress :) • i paint :) • reading <33 • Music is my number one that makes me feel great. • I Love To Film :) It makes me happy • Soccer:) • I just remember that I'm not living for anyone else but myself. & that I don't care what people think of me. :) • playing outside =) • You have the right to smile, so why not?

MichelleTells, age 18

YOU

are the best

ARTiST.

How are you
iNfluENCiNg yourSelf...
and your SPHeRe ?

Be a flawd Light in the WORLd

I won't judge you. I've been through some hard times myself so I can probably be of some help.

Couchpotatokid05, age 17

The voices in this book represent a generation:

GeNeRatioN
WE

the
FLawd
& PowerRful

WE are all about being done. Not almost done. Not kind of done. But very done. Overdone. Crispy done.

aka MilLeNNiaLs, global geNeRatioN, geneRation Next, the Net geNeRatioN

WE are done with Hate and everything that comes from it.

WE are sending hate out of our collective hearts and off the planet . . . while we still can.

What we have to do is stop. Let's stop the hate.
HannahTheDreamer100, age 15

Stop frickin' hate in this world.
MeghanProductions, age 16

It ends now.
ProjectCaritas, age 17

All we have to do is present another option. I think it is possible, and I really, really, really, really would love to look back and noticeably see that there's a shift in the way we treat each other and the way we treat ourselves.
Emily Greener (@ThatGirlGreener),
cofounder of I AM THAT GIRL

The writing is on the wall. And the ceiling. And the floors. And the windows. "WE are inheriting a world in decline, a damaged future, a set of catastrophic problems" . . . and the time has come to do something about it.

It actually came a long time ago, but nobody really did anything so . . . WE will.

according to GEN-WE.com

We Stop Hate. You know what it is, oh yeah. All teens coming together, telling their stories and hoping to help everybody around the world.

CorttneyDunkin, age 18

WE will
STOP as much
HATE as possible.

WE will
START as much
LOVE as possible.

As a citizen of the world I am also a servant to others. So the greatness I have to share should never be to be superior to someone else. It should only help unlock someone else's potential.

Alyson Stoner (@AlysonOnTour), age 20, *Cheaper by the Dozen*

WE are here to serve. And WE know it.

You're Ready.

If you're welling up with emotion as you read this, it's because you recognize something. Something that inspires the desire to step up . . . and put yourself out there . . . by being who you are . . . and sharing it, FULL-OUT!

You're Ready to be a flawd LIGHT in the WORLd.

Or maybe that's not how you're feeling right this minute. Maybe you're feeling pretty sure you don't have anything to share. Or what you have to share couldn't possibly make a difference. Or that you'll share later.

If you're feeling anything along those lines, it's likely because your old pal (and *my* old pal) Not Good Enough has inserted itself. Inserted itself to do its usual: Protect you from . . . what does it want to protect you from again? Oh yeah . . . dying a horrible, humiliating death.

Except . . .

Being saved from a horrible, humiliating death isn't what you (or I) want most right now. Shining is. So this is what you do . . .

Just as soon as you sense Not Good Enough's presence, you call it out.

Then, what you do next makes it kind of exciting that Not Good Enough has shown up. You get to Face It. You get to smile at it and say:

"I am PLeNty good enough."

Really chew up the scenery when you say the word "PLENTY."

"I am
Puhh-leN-tee
good enough."

You do not need to do or have one more thing happen to you to be good enough.

Fabulously flawd as you are, you are ready to shine!

In fact, let your old pal Not Good Enough in on this secret: You're ready to shine *because* you are flawd.

You, right now as you're [watching] this, you are enough. In this moment, today, tomorrow and forever just as you are.

TaylorrScreamsRawrr, age 15

• How to Be a Flawd Light 1 •
FLub UP

Yup. The way it really works is this: while Not Good Enough is trying to make you believe you're not ready to shine, the truth is that when you share your light *before* you get to "All Ready Land," *that* is when your TRUE best gets shared.

I'm talking about what people get from you when they see you trying really hard to do great things in the world and . . . you flub up.

People LOVE seeing other people flub up because they're so afraid of doing it themselves. And when they see you giving it your all and coming up short in one way or another (but then also seeing that you don't get zapped off the face of the earth as punishment for missing the mark), people feel like they've been given a real gift . . . the gift of permission. Permission to try hard, put themselves way out there, and should it happen . . . flub up.

> I'm still not perfect, nobody is.
> JillianLovesFilm, age 16

The only thing that's not okay about flubbing up is when you can't stand that it happened. Like I did all through middle school. I'd lie in bed every night, wasting energy re-playing the entire day, cringing about all the things I wish I had done differently.

To be okay with your flub-ups is to understand that life is messy — *messy, messy, MESS-YYY!* And that spills (both small and stupendous) are inevitable. Moving on from them with your flawd light still shining bright — that's not just beautiful and brave, it's the whole game.

Be you ...flubs, flaws, freak-outs and all.

Flubbing and loving yourself anyway makes you the best kind of be-YOU-tiful. It gives you back the beauty you were born with.

> On the day that you were born we all had to look away because your beauty was so powerful that if we'd looked directly at you at that perfect moment in time, we would've exploded. I would compare your beauty to the biggest plate of bacon and chocolate with a unicorn and a rainbow on top. Unless you're vegetarian. Which is still beautiful. So keep being beautiful.
>
> ItsAntoniaWithAnA, age 16

What if...

. . . instead of being **ashamed** of our flubs and flaws, we had **compassion** for them?

What if...

. . . instead of being **embarrassed** by our flubs and flaws, we had **curiosity** about them?

What if...

. . . instead of letting our flubs and flaws make us act **small**, we let them set us **free**?

• How to Be a Flawd Light 2 •

Do What you Love

My only tip for you guys is to find something you love and do that thing a lot. Like for me I found YouTube. I joined YouTube just because I was bored and then I started getting lots of really great comments, like you're funny and you're pretty and stuff and it really boosted my confidence. Look at me now, I'm a YouTube partner and things are going really great. Everyone's different so maybe YouTube isn't right for you, maybe it's a sport or drawing or something. I don't know, but just find something you love. I really do think it's easier to love yourself when you love what you're doing.

Unicornfunk123, age 16

Like the quote above from my friend Deidre (Unicornfunk123), I think it's a lot easier to love yourself when you love what you're doing. But doing what we love can get stopped in its tracks. By fear.

Fear of being made fun of.

Do you ever have that fear?

The fear that doing what you love will open you up to ridicule? It's a legitimate concern because when something as important to you as what you love gets ridiculed, it *hurts*. Ask my friend Ricky Dillon. When he started doing what he loves — making YouTube videos — that's exactly what happened:

> Last year in high school I made a video to "Move Along" by the All-American Rejects. It got sent around school somehow. My whole grade saw it. A lot of people were making fun of me. They were just calling me names, saying bad things about the video and bad things about me as a person. I just felt like the whole world was making fun of me. I finally realized I shouldn't let other people affect what I like to do, especially people I don't even talk to. My friends helped me realize that I should still keep doing what I'm doing — what I'm passionate about — and to not let those people affect that.

Ricky didn't let being made fun of stop him. And do you know what? Four years later he's one of the five members on the YouTube collab channel O2L (Our2ndLife).

FYI, O2L has over 3 million subscribers today.

Be like Ricky. Don't let the possibility of mean-spirited teasing stop you from doing what you're passionate about. What you're passionate about is your gift. Honor it.

Be proud of who you are. Express yourself through what you're passionate about. Keep doing it.
Ricky Dillon (@RickyPDillon), age 17, Internet personality

How to HONOR
the gift of
"What you ♥"

1. Do it
2. Share it
(a lot)

I'm working on my life philosophy right now, and so far what I have is this: Find the one thing that you think you're put here to do and then do it with all your heart. And then I think whatever that purpose is needs to be in service to others. Because there's a lot of energy that comes out of that. And if you do that, then you'll be leading a really fulfilled life.
Ashton Moio (@AshtonMoio), age 22, *The Hunger Games*

• How to Be a Flawd Light 3 •

Be you

It's so simple, it practically goes without saying: Be YOU.

But straightforward as "Be YOU" sounds, it's a very easy thing to get away from. That's why it's so impressive when being YOU happens.

Being YOU happens when you're doing the smallest, most ordinary, everyday things. But the smallest, most ordinary, everyday things are actually really big things. They're acts of bravery. Ordinary Acts of Bravery.

ORdiNaRy
acts of
BRaVERy
look like this...

- Making a video because that's your passion . . . even if it means getting cyberbullied.

- Not straightening your hair because you just don't want to anymore . . . even if it makes you less "fashionable."

- Giving somebody who's having a tough day a compliment . . . even though you're feeling shy yourself.

My mom likes to say, "Boys don't make passes at girls who wear glasses." I wear glasses anyway. Some of my friends say I shouldn't wear horizontal stripes, but I love them and wear them a lot. When it comes to fashion, I'm all about acts of bravery — and comfort!

And one of the best things about being brave enough to be YOU?

Being you is a Revolutionary act.

Being you is a way to celebrate the world as it was created: absurdly rich in diversity.

> The world needs to have everyone bringing their own piece to the table. The world needs the diversity.
>
> Corbin Bleu (@CorbinBleu), *High School Musical*

Being you is a way of standing for a world that knows how to be inclusive.

> No matter religion, race, gender, sexual orientation. We are just people that want to be loved and that want to be happy.
>
> ProjectCaritas, age 17

Being you votes for a world that can see humor + intelligence + beauty in the unconventional . . . and the ordinary.

> People who have freckles, most of the time they don't really like them, and if you have freckles, play up your freckles.
>
> BowBeauty24, age 18

• How to Be a Flawd Light 4 •

Be for Something

Being *for* something is best because of how it inspires and uplifts and unifies and generally gives you energy. Being *for* something can also be sustained.

Being *against* something? It's none of that.

> I know that it's easier said than done, not to focus on negative aspects about yourself or on negative things that are occurring in the world, but I have learned that the more that I focus on positive things or things that I actually like about myself, it seems like everything else around me is just easier.
>
> Shane Bitney Crone (@ShaneBitney), *Bridgegroom*

It's easy to be against stuff. We do it all the time as though it's our best option. But have you ever noticed how you take on the worst aspects of what you're against? As though it's okay to bear intolerance, resistance, anger, combativeness, one-upmanship if it supports your beliefs about what's wrong.

Fortunately, being against things is extremely draining and can't be sustained. This is very good because it prevents you from going too far down that road. If you are on the "against" road in relation to something you care about right now, maybe this will help turn you around:

The best
Being against something
will ever do is
change it.

While

Being FOR something

has the power

to TRANSFORM it.

If it's something that really matters to you, don't waste your time with change. Upgrade to transformation. Because at this point in human history, it's only transformation that's going to cut it. The extreme-makeover-no-messin'-around-balls-to-the-wall-take-no-prisoners variety.

I happen to be against hate and harm. Turn that inside out and you've got love and help. That's why I'm all about helping others to feel good about themselves.

How about you? Do you know what you're for?

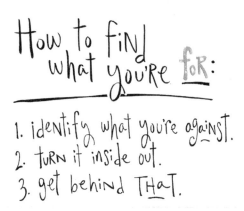

How to find
what you're for:

1. identify what you're against.
2. turn it inside out.
3. get behind THAT.

• How to Be a Flawd Light 5 •

Remember

We're all guilty of forgetting the best stuff all the time. That's why reminders are the secret to life.

ReMiNDeRs
CReate them • Post them •
Lots of them.
all over the Place.

The better the reminders, the more you remember to shine your flawd light out into the world. People have all kinds of creative ways to remind themselves of the most important things.

Give yourself reminders. If you use your history book a lot in school, put a little reminder in your history book that says, "I am beautiful. I am worth it. I am perfectly imperfect, and that's all I need to be and have to be."

BowBeauty24, age 18

I really like my WeStopHate bracelet. Every time I look at it, it reminds me I am who I am and people can judge me if they want to but it really doesn't matter.

JJWebShows101, age 15

Me? I love inspirational quotes so I use them as reminders. My most important thing to remember is taped to my bathroom mirror. I found this quote when I was struggling with anxiety in high school, and it resonated with me. I now read it every day while brushing (and flossing).

I share it with you now hoping it can help us all remember how to let ourselves — fabulously flawd and full of light as we are — shine bright for all the world to see, no matter what.

Finish each day
and be done with it.
You have done what you could.
Some blunders and absurdities
no doubt crept in;
forget them as soon as you can.
Tomorrow is a new day;
begin it well and serenely
and with too high a spirit
to be encumbered with
old nonsense.

– Ralph Waldo Emerson

Everyone in this world is a beautiful person. You just really need to be yourself and you need to just really not care what other people think. It's pretty simple and I feel like eventually if everyone finally gets out of their brainwashed self, they can realize there doesn't need to be hate in this world. We can all be happy, we can all get along.

Because this is WeStopHate on YouTube and this is what it's all about. So throw these tips in your head and don't hate on someone, don't let people lower your self-esteem, just be yourself and see what happens.

Have a nice day, guys. Bye.

DeeFizzy, age 17

One Final Thought...

Running WeStopHate and working with the WeStopHate team has been the most rewarding experience of my life. I encourage all of you to use your flawd light to take a stand about something you care about. More than anything, my biggest advice is this:

JUST START.

CHAPTER 1

"We mistake ourselves for our stories. We have stories, but we are NOT our stories."

Mark Matousek is a (bestselling) writer I'm proud to call a friend. He teaches the transformative power of writing for personal awakening. A lot of the ideas around "Who Am I?" are courtesy of his influence on my thinking. Whether you're interested in writing or not, check out all that's offered at MarkMatousek.com.

Keep the Game Going!

James P. Carse wrote an extraordinary book called *Finite and Infinite Games: A Vision of Life as Play and Possibility*. That's where I learned the "infinite games" approach to life and it's made such a difference. *"A finite game is played for the purpose of winning, an infinite game for the purpose of continuing the play."*

Ready? Set . . . Blab

The Artist's Way by Julia Cameron is a classic. Her version of "Ready? Set . . . BLAB" is called "Morning Pages." Well worth reading her version.

CHAPTER 2

How you see *yourself* is how you see *everything*.

My ability to say things like this with so much assurance comes from reading and reflecting on what Deepak Chopra, Debbie Ford, and Marianne Williamson say in *The Shadow Effect: Illuminating the Hidden Power of Your True Self.* I found Debbie Ford's take on things to be especially helpful.

10,000 Hours

Even though everyone references 10,000 hours now, it was Malcolm Gladwell who introduced us to 10,000 hours in *Outliers.*

The Art Version of Perspective

This take on perspective came to me while on a tear listening to all of Alain de Botton's YouTube videos. Don't ask me which video it was in now. I recommend you go on the same tear and watch everything of his.

CHAPTER 3

Ask "What If . . . ?"

"What If" was inspired by "The Magic If" — a technique the Russian actor-director Constantin Stanislavski (1863–1938) came up with to train actors. He knew that only a crazy person could believe that he was *really* in the event he was acting out onstage, so Stanislavski gave his actors "If" as a tool for finding their way into the *possibility* of the events . . . and to act the heck out of the scene without being crazy.

Stay Put . . . in the Present

Mindfulness is all the rage now so there's a ton and a half out there to read about it. Present moment awareness is the always-available soothing balm your nervous system needs to counteract so much online time. Go learn more about it (online if you must) . . . and then actually, really do it (offline).

CHAPTER 4

Columbus-ing

Acknowledging revisionist (untrue) history is one of the issues of our time. It's finally happening and it's necessary if we're really interested in stopping hate. We cannot transform what we cannot acknowledge. We need to be fearless and humble about telling it like it really was. How it really was is what gave rise to how it really is. It's painful, but I learned a lot about how it really was from Howard Zinn's *A People's History of the United States*.

CHAPTER 5

Honeybees Dying

In her 2013 TED Talk, "Why Bees Are Disappearing," Marla Spivak says, *"Honeybees have thrived for 50 million years, each colony 40 to 50,000 individuals coordinated in amazing harmony. So why, seven years ago, did colonies start dying en masse?"* Then she lays out four reasons why.

CHAPTER 6

Whom You Surround Yourself With

Sorry. I conflated two Buddha stories. Buddha did, in fact, tell Ananda, "*Admirable friendship, admirable companionship, admirable camaraderie is actually the whole of the holy life*" (Upaddha Sutta), but not on his deathbed (Maha-parinibbana Sutta). I almost changed it when I found out, but I think my telling of it is so good, I'd rather they rearrange the original discourses to match mine.

Virtues and Signature Strengths

I learned a lot when I came across Christopher Peterson and the VIA Classification of Character Strengths just noodling around online. His book, *A Primer in Positive Psychology*, is said to be the best introduction to positive psychology ever written because it's fun to read and it makes you feel smart. I haven't yet, but I'm going to read it.

Influence = Power

Daniel Goleman is the godfather of emotional intelligence. He wrote the book on it. Literally. In his YouTube video "The Future of Leadership," he lays out why influence is the new power . . . and how that makes us all leaders.

The Ripple Effect

Thomas Morgan is the producer of the documentary *Storied Streets: Reframing the Way You See Homelessness*. In his 2013 TED

Talk, "Put On Your Underoos, It's Time to Save the World," he talks about the amazingness of the Ripple Effect in a way that made me want to see what I could do with it.

CHAPTER 7

"WE are inheriting a world in decline, a damaged future, a set of catastrophic problems . . ."

GEN-WE.com talks about what's so very unfortunate about the world young people are stepping into in ways that will leave you feeling hopeful. They face it with bright yet sober "we got this" energy.

I Am Plenty Good Enough

In his talk on "The Healing Power of Mindfulness," Jon Kabat-Zinn said something that anchored "I'm *plenty* good enough" in me once and for all. He said, "*If you hope it, then make it happen. It lies with YOU. If you want the education of the future to be different, don't look around for someone else to do it. YOU do it. When will you be good enough? NEVER. Because part of your mind will tell you you don't have enough power; you don't have enough influence; you don't have enough . . . this. You've got PLENTY. You can take the initiative.*"

Flub Up

Once (well, not just once) I made a fool of myself in front of a lot of people. I recounted the horror of my flubbed performance to art teacher Frank Young. He said, "*You wanted to be a star, but you were something much better. You were a service.*" He considered it a service because seeing imperfection in others makes people feel less alone with their own fears of inadequacy.

Being You Is a Revolutionary Act

Inspired by a line in Chris Rock's 2009 documentary, *Good Hair* — an exploration of the ways hairstyles impact the black community. Tracie Thoms said, "*To keep my hair the same texture as it grows out of my head is looked at as revolutionary. Why is that?*"

Be for Something

Adyashanti, a hip (but more important, clear) American-born spiritual teacher, spoke eloquently about "*What am I in service to? And what's the wisest way to go about it?*" If you put Adyashanti and Omega Institute (where he was when he said it) into the search bar, you'll find it.

The Conspicuously Absent Brené Brown

"No Brené Brown while writing *FLAWD*" was a very conscious decision. The reminder, "It's already been done . . . by a rock star!" would have stopped me in my tracks. Fortunately, what Brené has (so generously) contributed to the flawd conversation is now in our collective unconscious and I was able to pull from that. But now that *FLAWD* is written, I'm listening to her book *The Gifts of Imperfection* . . . and you should too!

• ACKNOWLEDGMENTS •

FIRST AND FOREMOST, thank you to Jeanne Demers. We wouldn't be holding this book without you. When it comes to my most important "other people," your flawd light shines bright. Schmid needs her Ruby.

Thank you to Jess Weiner for inspiring me, always. My life was forever changed once you entered. Lori Majewski for believing in that fifteen-year-old go-getter, and Seth Matlins, Eric Dawson, Jennifer Barkley, Jason Feldman, Nathalie Molina Niño, Shane Pollack, Nanette DiLauro, Anita and John Magliola, Monique Coleman, Denise Restauri, and Lady Gaga for investing so much of your time, energy, and resources into my growth and development.

Thank you to Brandon Turley, Jillian Carney, Kaitlyn Moorhead, Sam Kielmanowicz, Deidre Mollura, and Claire Lawlor. Working and collaborating with you has been the most rewarding part of WeStopHate. Thank you to Eden Sher, Kaleb Nation, and Alexa Losey for helping bring my LA vision to life.

It is my friends who continuously leave footprints on my heart. Nathizzz, you'll always be Schmiddlebopper's Numero Uno. And Schmiddlebopper would be nothing without her Boppers. To all my initial Boppers, thank you — my YouTube and WeStopHate journey would not have been possible without you. Lastly, thank you to my incredible friends at Convent of the Sacred Heart in Greenwich,

Connecticut. Going through middle school with you transformed me from the ostracized bullying victim into the confident, self-assured woman I am today.

I wouldn't be where I am without the support and love I receive on an ongoing basis from We Are Family Foundation (for truly being my social change *family*), Peace First (for helping me see that I am a peacemaker), Do Something (for exposing me to teen activists), and the Body Shop (for coloring my world beautiful).

When it comes to my family, I love you with my whole heart. Thank you to my mom, who makes me feel unconditionally loved, always. To my papa for teaching me the lessons and values I hold most dear. To Jacquie for your loving generosity in every aspect of my life, Ava for all our heart-to-hearts, Selam for loving me as your own, Mimi and Bear and Papasmommy for being such loving grandparents. There is no question that I won the birth lottery.

Emily-Anne Rigal

❦   ❦   ❦

THANKS FIRST GO to Emily-Anne Rigal, for our friendship. I love our friendship. Thank you for trusting me with this project and for being a laugh-riot to work with. Career dream come true, my flawd friend forever.

I speak for both of us when I say thank you, Lisa DiMona. You are an amazing agent! Thank you for always going to bat for us in a big way.

I speak for both of us, too, when I thank Penguin Perigee for bringing us into the fold, and for giving us all the creative freedom we could ever want. We are so fortunate to have John Duff, a publisher who makes us feel like gold. Meg Leder, our (very) high-end and (very) down-to-earth editor on the rise. Jeanette Shaw, our fourth-quarter, superstar editor. A dream team of an art and production department — thank you, Kellie Schirmer and Tiffany Estreicher and Jennifer Eck and Nellys Liang. The fine eye of our copyeditor, Joan Matthews. The inspired marketing team, too. Thank you all for your belief, love, and support!

So many have contributed to making this flawd gift possible. I speak of my influences. The first thing I think of to thank is P-Funk. Philosophically, *FLAWD* funks around. *"Faults, defects or shortcomings? . . . I want you to lay it on your radio."*

I look up from writing and say "Thank you" to the lake I grew up on . . . and came back to . . . to work on this book. Mousam Lake in Acton, Maine, "Thank you."

I thank my family. All around me, cheering me on with so many "O'Jeanne!" hugs as I wrote. Thank you, dear Demers Family, one and all.

I thank my wise council of friends. Mark Matousek, your generosity is a thing of beauty. "Oh, *use* it," of everything you expounded on when asked . . . Wise Women: Susanna Brackman, Ruth Cook, Cis Wilson, Cynthia Adler, Rita Schwartz, Michelle Gutman, Ellen Schecter, Deborah Kampmeier, Claire Unsinn, Terri Haas, Laura Fasano, Silvia Vassao, Rita Cassie. Wise Men: Joseph, foremost, for the decades of pep talks. Frank Young, Peter Iannarelli, Ed Murr. All of my Beacon, New York peeps, with an especially deep bow to Rob Penner for all things helpful *at all times*.

Jean Cocteau Repertory for putting language in my body.

Mentors Marty and Helene and Leonard and Oonaja for Life 101-LOL. Architect Cary Cook for the alphabet. Screenwriter Ziggy Steinberg for the inside line on story and comedy (B and P are funny, T is not funny).

(If this were my Academy Award speech, the music would be turning up right now to get me offstage . . .) *Thank you, ALL!* Oh, one more before I go . . .

Thank you, IMS, thank you, dharma!

Thank you, nearest-and-dearest Diane Rooney, Suki and Danielle and Tim, the incomparable Lian Amber, the Facebook cheering section, and — (the music's loud now so I'm yelling . . .)

And Brené Brown! For goodness' sake, Brené Brown!

And YOU, thank YOU, for YOU. Really, thank YOU.

Jeanne Demers